The Power of Two: Partner Teams in Action

by

Penny Bishop and Garet Allen-Malley

National Middle School Association

Westerville, Ohio

National Middle School Association
4151 Executive Parkway, Suite 300
Westerville, Ohio 43081
Telephone: (800) 528-NMSA
NMSA www.nmsa.org

Sue Swaim, Executive Director
Jeff Ward, Associate Executive Director
Edward Brazee, Editor, Professional Publications
John Lounsbury, Consulting Editor, Professional Publications
April Tibbles, Director of Publications
Dawn Williams, Production Specialist
Mark Shumaker, Graphic Designer
Mary Mitchell, Designer, Editorial Assistant
Marcia Meade-Hurst, Senior Publications Representative

Library of Congress Cataloging-in-Publication Data
Bishop, Penny, date
    The power of two: partner teams in action/by Penny Bishop
        and Garet-Allen Malley. p. cm.
    Includes bibliographical references.
    ISBN: 1-56090-147-0 (pbk.)
    1. Teaching teams--United States. 2. Middle Schools--
United States. 3. Interdisciplinary approach in education--
United States. I. Allen-Malley, Garet. II. Title.

LB1029.T4B57 2004
373.11'48--dc22   2004042670

TABLE OF CONTENTS

ABOUT THE AUTHORS

Penny Bishop, who began her career as a middle grades teacher before serving as assessment consultant for the Vermont Department of Education, is currently an assistant professor at the University of Vermont where she directs the middle level teacher education program. Dr. Bishop, who is active professionally, has research interests in partner teaming, current issues in initial teacher preparation, and student perceptions of academic engagement. Her dissertation on partner teaming received the 1998 Distinguished Dissertation Award from the National Association of Secondary School Principals.

Garet Allen-Malley has been involved in Vermont education since 1976. A former classroom teacher, special educator, and middle and high school curriculum coordinator, she also served at the Vermont Department of Education as a consultant for learning disabilities and technical advisor for special education. Dr. Allen-Malley is currently a lecturer in the middle level teacher education program at the University of Vermont with special interests in teaming and reading across the curriculum.

FOREWORD

*It's easy to get good players. Getting 'em to play
together is the hard part.* — Casey Stengel

Indeed.

Perhaps the most notable change over the last three decades in
how middle schools are best organized for young adolescent learners
and their teachers has been a reorganization into interdisciplinary
teams. This structural change offered a promising opportunity for
educators to achieve the overarching goal of the middle school
movement, namely *schooling based on the nature and needs of
young adolescents*. Many if not most schools at this level transitioned
from the strict departmental organization of the junior high school
to subsets of the full school, with teams comprised of 100 to 125
students served by four or more teachers, each representing an
academic specialty. It became common for school officials to then
rename their buildings middle schools.

While the teaming initiative became the initial and essential
change in the emergence of the middle school concept, it gradually
became clear that although teams appeared to serve everyone better
than departmentalization, the goal of fully meeting student needs
remained elusive. Even with smaller communities of students
and teachers — schools within a school, so to speak — the primary
enterprise of teaching and learning did not change appreciably. Once
the appealing novelty of team configurations wore off, to a large
extent practice often reverted to familiar patterns and pedagogy.
As Casey Stengel observed above, getting them to play together
was indeed the hard part. Teacher advisory programs were devised
to assure students an adult advocate, but owing to high ratios of

students to teachers and brief fixed meeting times in a complex schedule, teachers' intentions to know and guide every student well enough to accommodate individual differences were frustrated.

Meanwhile, small schools—often in villages and rural areas—had to modify the teaming concept to fit their circumstances. Many schools had such small student populations that they could not provide a separate teacher for every subject area. Often there would be just a handful of students at each grade level, so grouping horizontally by age and grade wasn't feasible. In such cases necessity became the mother of invention. Teams took on several unique features: students from two or three grade levels were grouped together to have enough people to constitute a team; two or three teachers would be assigned to these multigrade teams to teach all of the core subjects; teachers took responsibilities for much of the schedule, grouping, and other administrative duties within the team. These novel teams enabled teachers and students to work together for longer than a single year, and at least some portions of the curriculum were combined along the lines of interdisciplinary and integrated studies. It is evident, even to the casual visitor, however, that many elements in these smaller, unique teams function very effectively, and it is the exploration of these elements that Penny Bishop and Garet Allen-Malley describe insightfully in this volume.

The modifier of *partner* deserves special attention when used to describe a team. The key element in such teams is the achievement of partnership—a collaboration that involves the three central constituencies in every school: teachers, students, parents. The essential partnership that must be formed from the very beginning concerns the two teachers who work closely together to invent and sustain the educational program for the team. A second dimension of partnership is between the teachers and their students; exemplary teams such as those described in this book are true communities of adults and children in which students have an active voice in their education. The third partnership is between the two adult constituencies—teachers and parents. When teachers and parents work well together, the children who are the objects of their efforts also thrive. When professional decisions and programs rest on this tripodic configuration, the potential for achieving a relevant, coherent educational experience for all students is great, and it accommodates the nature and needs of young adolescent students more fully than any other known model.

The indispensable union in every partner team is between the teachers, and the necessary condition each individual teacher needs from the partnership is the personal efficacy that brings self-confidence and foments continued personal and professional growth. Mutual support, decision making, professional development, reflective practice, risk taking, and the simple enjoyment of teaching that characterize partner teaming are richly detailed in this book. Its scenarios portray teachers who work harmoniously and comfortably with one another. Their daily work reflects a continuity and consistency that extends over time, ensuring their students' feelings of safety and predictability about their program. The reader cannot avoid being impressed by the mutual support teachers provide for each other as well as to their students and parents. The sense of a vigorous, healthy, family-like community is unmistakable.

Middle level teachers especially benefit when they inquire seriously and earnestly into what their students need and want from schooling. My experience is that when kids feel trusted and listened to, they tell it like it truly is. Such inquiries are sure to show that students need to feel a strong sense of belonging and connection with each other, their teachers, and to their primary group, in this case to their team. Relationships are everything to young adolescents, and without the assurance of friends and caring teachers, little learning is likely to occur. This book includes ample evidence of teams that have achieved just such an interpersonal climate, often using touching anecdotes that project the quality of mutual respect and caring that characterizes interpersonal relationships within teams. Partner teams can be true cradles of participatory democracy.

This distinctive volume also reports what parents seek and value in their children's middle level schooling. Parent concerns that at least one adult at the school knows, cares about, and looks after their child is more than met in partner teams where every student is known well by the two core teachers. Teachers' sensitivity to parents' concerns and urgent issues is described in more than one instance. Parents' participation in curricular, social, and recreational activities is also illustrated. As a parent and grandparent, I would feel very fortunate to have any member of my family associated with these teams. I would rest assured that teachers would work conscientiously to create learning opportunities in which the personal and intellectual capacities of my children or grandchildren would be cultivated and celebrated. What a wonderful world of schooling we would have accomplished if every parent could make this assertion!

The eminent anthropologist, Margaret Mead, once observed, "A small group of committed people can change the world. And, indeed, it is the only thing that ever does." Professor Mead once visited a school at which middle level students were formed in partner teams. She wanted to see for herself just how young adolescents went about their daily lives and studies. She asked the teachers penetrating questions about team communication and the system of accountability devised to document student learning, and she patiently reviewed samples of student work. Finally, she randomly asked students to talk to her about themselves, their interests and skills, and their thoughts about their team. Apparently satisfied with what she learned, Dr. Mead shortly thereafter enrolled her young granddaughter in the school, expressing her eager anticipation that she would soon be old enough to be part of a middle level partner team. I know this anecdote to be true, because I was one of the three teachers on that team in 1973, and I hosted her visits and responded to her questions. In that partner team, as in the ones described in this book, a small group of committed people—adults and children—had created an educational world for themselves that constituted an authentic advancement beyond the conventional that more nearly accommodated the nature and needs of young adolescent students, their teachers, and their parents. Bishop and Allen-Malley are to be commended for leading us into the essence and intricacies of what is hoped to become the next significant evolutionary stage in the middle level concept.

Chris Stevenson
Pinehurst, North Carolina

1

THE CASE FOR PARTNER TEAMS

*Small schools come as close to being a panacea for
America's educational ills as we're likely to get.
Smallness is a prerequisite for the climate and culture
that we need to develop the habits of the heart and
mind essential to a democracy. Such a culture emerges
from authentic relationships built on face-to-face
conversations by people engaged in common work and
common work standards.* — Deborah Meier, 1996

Schools are inherently social places. When asked to visualize
"school," most people quickly conjure up an image of a noisy
hallway filled with moving bodies and laughter or a particular
class and either a respected or a disliked teacher. Indeed, the story of
education is a story of relationships. Ask a person to describe his or
her most important memories, and the stories one most often hears
detail teachers and peers and the ways they interacted. Rarely do the
memories reflect specific academic learnings; when they do, these
learnings are typically through a relationship, as a person describes
how one special teacher opened his or her eyes to the power of
poetry, or the awesome symmetry in nature, or his or her own self-
worth.

For middle level teachers, this story of relationships is inten-
sified. Not only do they work with between 50 and 125 students each
day as members of interdisciplinary teams, they find themselves

intricately connected to colleagues, negotiating the multitude of tasks that teaching inevitably includes. "Teaming" has emerged as the key term in middle schools and is used to describe various configurations, from a pair of educators teaching one group of learners to as many as five teachers planning and implementing learning for over 100 students. With roots at least as far back as the Eight-Year Study in the 1930s (Aikin, 1942), the concept of team organization has been expanded and refined by the middle level movement. Over the past few decades, middle level experts have advocated teaming as a prime feature of successful middle level programs. The practice is associated with the presence of common planning and teaching time and with attempts to integrate the more traditionally segregated curriculum.

The evolution of teaming

The extent of interdisciplinary team organization within our nation's middle level schools has increased substantially, growing from 30 percent in 1988, to 52 percent in 1993, and again all the way to 77 percent in 2001 (McEwin, Dickinson, & Jenkins, 2003). Teaming in middle level schools has now become the norm.

The Carnegie Corporation states in its second report of the task force on education of young adolescents, "Creating smaller schools is an important strategy for fostering supportive relationships between teachers and students. In large schools or small, however, creating teams of teachers and students is a vital part of developing a middle grades learning community" (Jackson & Davis, 2000, p. 125). National Middle School Association's position paper, *This We Believe: Successful Schools for Young Adolescents* (2003) identified as one of 14 key characteristics of successful middle schools, "Organizational structures that support meaningful relationships and learning" (p. 29). In delineating that characteristic, the paper claims, "the interdisciplinary team of two to four teachers working with a common group of students is the signature component of high-performing schools, literally the heart of the school from which other desirable programs and experiences evolve" (p. 29). And further, the paper claims, "Teaming is the starting place for building a strong learning community with its sense of family, where students and teachers know one another well, feel safe and supported, and are encouraged to take intellectual risks" (p. 29). State-wide initiatives provide similar commitments to interdisciplinary team organization. The Vermont Middle Grades Task Force Report (2001) recommends: "Students in the middle grades should be served by interdisciplinary teams of two or more teachers who share a common group of students for one or more years" (p. 18). The Georgia Alliance for Middle Level Excellence (n.d.) has called for "interdisciplinary teams of teachers with adequate common planning time to devote to meeting the instructional needs of students." And the report of the Maine Commission on Middle Level Education (in press) states: "In successful middle schools, there is a strong sense of community established through smaller teams of two or three teachers and no more than 40-75 students. When these teams stay together for the two or three years that students are in middle school, strong relationships are formed, and a sense of belonging is fostered." With widespread endorsements of teaming as an essential component of developmentally responsive middle schools, and with policies being shaped by these endorsements, it is important to understand the research and practice pertaining to teaming.

Teaming outcomes and problems

Educators have embraced teaming, because it just makes sense; yet there is substantial research to support the practice. Teachers on middle school teams experience a sense of community and shared commitment that junior high teachers do not. For example, in investigating teachers' sense of efficacy in both a teamed middle school and a departmentalized junior high school, Ashton and Webb (1986) revealed the critical roles of three important factors; collaborative planning, teacher participation in school decision making, and extended blocks of teaching time—each likely to have positive effects. Teachers in collaborative environments come to feel a greater sense of satisfaction and efficacy and believe that they make a difference. Higher levels of collegiality, less stress, and enhanced articulation of curriculum also result from teaming.

Other research studies and cumulative experience are equally compelling in identifying ways students benefit from teaming. Increased student achievement has been found to be related to teachers' beliefs in both the efficacy of teaming as a whole and of their personal sense of efficacy. Ashton and Webb (1986) concluded that teachers with a strong sense of efficacy created a classroom climate that was warm and responsive to student needs, and students of such teachers tended to feel secure and scored higher on achievement tests than did the students of teachers with a lower sense of efficacy. Lee and Smith (1993) found that students in restructured middle schools—defined by less departmentalization, more team teaching, and other restructuring factors—scored significantly higher on both achievement and engagement measures than did students in non-restructured, or "traditional" junior high schools. Nor are benefits for students limited to the academic. As implied above, students on teams have a high sense of belonging, more positive attitudes toward school, and improved attendance.

Although the literature paints a positive picture of teaming, many educators have raised questions regarding the current status of teaming in middle schools. Some teachers feel only a limited level of comfort in interdisciplinary teaming, and few teams use common planning time regularly and effectively (Epstein & Mac Iver, 1990). Another study revealed that the responsibility for large numbers of students may inhibit teachers' ability to attend to individual students (McPartland, 1987). Considering the bulk of research and policy documents recommending the implementation of teams, these findings highlight the need to better understand the effectiveness of all teaming configurations. Since teaming is beneficial to students and teachers, and because teachers have not always capitalized on what teaming makes possible, we must learn from the dynamics of effective teams and consider alternatives to the larger four- or five-member interdisciplinary team that serves over 100 students. The question then, "Does partner teaming provide a viable and effective alternative?" merits serious consideration.

Smaller teams

The partner team is a potentially powerful alternative to the four- or five-teacher interdisciplinary team. A small, but emerging body of literature reports high degrees of effectiveness and teacher satisfaction on smaller teams (Alexander, 1995; Allen-Malley & Bishop, 2000; Arnold & Stevenson, 1998; Baltzer, 1995; Bishop & Stevenson, 2000; Springer, 1994). Summarizing research findings from longitudinal data collected from 70 middle schools, Flowers, Mertens, and Mulhall (2000) state, "Clearly smaller teams are better able to manage not only the team coordination that is necessary for best practices, but also the classroom practices that serve to implement the programs" (p. 56). These studies and advocacies make it important to understand fully the partner team as a prime alternative to its larger counterparts.

> There are, of course, successful larger teams, but there is a marked tendency for such teams to divide the day into periods of less than an hour and teach their subjects separately, thus replicating the junior high school departmental format that deters curriculum integration. We suspect that teaming in general and curriculum integration have not advanced as quickly as one would hope is in no small part because of the preponderance of large teams.
>
> (Arnold & Stevenson, 1998, p. 10)

Arnold and Stevenson's suspicion, widely supported by others, that the full implementation of teaming possibilities has been slow to develop due in part to the awkwardness of the larger team warrants serious study. The partner team appears to be an effective alternative and is almost certain to become more common in practice.

Although some smaller teams have been in existence throughout the middle level movement (Alexander, 1995; Springer, 1994), many have more recently developed out of a need to find more effective, satisfying ways to facilitate teaching and learning. In addition to having considerably fewer students, partner teams better use the longer block of instructional time. Baltzer (1995) describes greater curriculum integration on two-person partner teams, suggesting that attaining this level of collaboration "would be difficult on larger teams and impossible in a departmentalized setting" (p. 17). Baltzer also cites a positive effect on the students' transition from elementary school and a greater emphasis on affective goals as additional advantages of partner teaming. Alexander (1995) also identifies many benefits to the two-teacher team, including ease of scheduling, fostering close student-teacher relationships, and shared decision making.

Our research into partner teaming stemmed from a desire to better understand those teams that were providing powerful learning experiences for both teachers and students. Through interviews and extensive participant observation, we sought to understand what lay at the heart of the effective partner team. We wondered, *What do partner teachers view as the professional outcomes of their collaborative work? What are the benefits for students? What attributes do the team members possess? What is distinctive about their instruction? And what supports need to be in place to facilitate and sustain a partner team's effectiveness?* Answers to these and related questions hold important implications both for teachers and those in leadership positions who form or work with teams. Answers should help to ensure that other partner teams work effectively and reap the benefits that research and practice tell us teaming can bring to middle level education. And likewise, we hope to encourage the formation of new partner teams. Further, we assert, many of the findings underscored by the teachers cited in this book have implications beyond the middle level. The effective partner team speaks to the fundamentals of collaborative work and holds meaning for teachers at any level, from the pre-school classroom to the university setting.

The research that informs this book is based on two separate qualitative studies into the structure of middle level partner teaming. Both examined what teachers perceived as critical for their effectiveness in teaming. We present in this volume the voices and actions of eight partner teams from across New England, and we thank them for their participation. As detailed in the chart on page 7, they represented a range of teaching and teaming experience as well as teacher gender, student grade level, and building configuration.

To ensure confidentiality, the teachers' names used throughout this text are pseudonyms. While certainly there is much to celebrate in these teachers' practices, and most of the teachers would have been pleased to have their actual names used during the studies, all were highly sensitive to the need to ensure the anonymity of their students, particularly in controversial situations. To this end, the actual names of the schools, the partner teachers, and the young adolescents have not been used.

To understand what made these teams click, we interviewed teachers and students, observed and participated on teams extensively over time, and reviewed pertinent team and school documents to verify or call into question our initial findings. Through

Name	Years of teaching experience	Years teaming with present partner	# of students on team	Grades on Team	Grades in School
Hope	7	7	49	5-6	5-8
Krista	23				
Shannon	10	7	34	7	7-12
Erica	26				
John	19	2	56	6	K-8
Ted	17				
Heather	21	9	34	6	6-8
Alan	22				
Betsy	7	3	40	5-6	5-8
Sarah	28				
Rob	27	3	41	7-8	7-12
Ed	8				
Lori	5	3	39	7-8	7-12
Yvonne	21				
Nancy	27	6	36	5-6	K-6
Angie	6				

these processes, we came to understand what teachers and students perceived as the outcomes of such a team organization. We also uncovered valuable information and ideas about what is important to consider when forming teams and how to nurture and support a partner team.

In the pages that follow we represent these teams in two ways. First, within the chapters, we rely heavily on the voices of teachers and occasionally students to share the common themes that emerged from the studies. Believing that knowledge of teaching and learning resides within the teacher and learner, we present significant excerpts from interviews as a means to honor this expertise. Second, we intersperse narrative vignettes between the chapters that depict "days in the life" (Wolcott, 1994) of four of the eight partner teams, to further illustrate the negotiation and collaboration at play and to bring the reader directly into the classroom, to the heart of the action.

This book seeks to share with others the qualities and characteristics of effective partner teams. The rationale behind it is equally straightforward: Understanding examples of excellence helps us to strengthen our own approaches. Isn't this precisely why we provide our students with models or exemplars? Although the purpose and rationale are simple, the dynamics of the middle level partner teams portrayed in this book are, in fact, anything but. On the contrary, they consist of deeply embedded beliefs, personal attributes, and complex patterns of behavior that combine to form a team of two teachers who make magic in the classroom. In the pages that follow, we illustrate both what that magic looks like through the vignettes of four teams and how it happens through considerable analysis of teachers' perceptions and voices. ☺

TED AND JOHN

At 7:15 Monday morning, Ted pulls into the parking lot and then enters the newly renovated building, winding his way with long-legged strides down the corridor to the space which houses his team of sixth graders. He turns on the light, folds his green windbreaker, places it next to his desk, and begins the task of getting the room ready for the day. A technologically rich classroom in comparison to many in this rural landscape, the room boasts a total of nine computers, as well as a VCR that is hooked up to two television screens, one on each side of the wide classroom. He and his partner, John, have written many grants to receive this technological support and are proud of the resources they have secured for students. Ted begins booting up the computers and posting class jobs on the white board in the back of the room. He shuffles the index cards of student names, placing a new student in charge of tasks such as cleaning the computer screens, emptying the hole punch, and taking responsibility for recycling for the week. He adds to the existing list of "programs now available" on the white board—additional computer programs that students may use during their morning computer time, a time that rotates throughout the year to ensure all students have opportunities to work with technology.

As students begin to drift in, Ted possesses a quiet, confident, and respectful manner as he interacts with them. Several students approach him with requests.

"Can I go return these to the library?"

"Do you have an extra portfolio problem I can do?"

"Mr. D., do you have last night's paper? Did you read about the hockey player getting his 50th goal?"

Ted takes care of the requests quickly and matter-of-factly, while at the same time managing to be attentive to the hockey conversation so obviously important to the one student.

His partner John arrives, talking and joking with some students who are gathered around him. He sets his briefcase down and takes off his coat. By this time, most of their 56 students are seated. He looks over at Ted; they smile, exchange knowing glances, and laugh without speaking a word. Their desks sit side by side as a divider between the general classroom desk space and the computers. Ted comes over with a piece of paper in hand

and discusses with John the changes in their schedule because of parent conferences. Although they held parent conferences last week, several parents were unable to attend at that time. They are now fitting them into lunch times, preparation times, and after school on several days this week in order to accommodate them. John takes the note from Ted, hole-punches it, and places it in one of their many team binders.

"Mr. D, something's wrong!" Their conversation is interrupted by a concerned student on one of the computers. Ted suggests a course of action for the student, and his solution rights the problem quickly.

"Okay, why don't we all sit down? I know several of you have spelling to work on," Ted addresses the class. Most students take their seats at their desks, talking quietly; the remainder continue to enjoy computer time. This first half-hour of the day is dedicated to a variety of tasks, including this rotating computer time. Some students work on late homework; others complete their class jobs; still others enjoy the opportunity to read quietly.

"I think Mr. D said some of you should be working on your spelling; others can read," John reminds the students of their options. He turns to a girl near him, and asks, "Would you put all this material from the box into different piles? It's for Boating Safety; it finally came in." With his hands full, he is approached by another student who asks if she might have a pass to the library to return her books. "The library? Go see Mr. D." Ted watches this interaction, and laughs, "Did he pass the buck? Okay. That's my job."

John addresses the class, "Okay. This is for attendance and lunch." He proceeds to call their names, and the students answer loudly as their names are called with responses like, "Hot!", and "Milk!", and "Nothing!" Ted circulates while John completes this task. Ted moves on to remind students of the class jobs for the week, reading off the name changes. Abruptly, a student voice comes over the intercom, reading announcements and leading them in the Pledge of Allegiance. The phone rings shortly thereafter, and John answers, gives a short, "Okey dokey. Very good. Bye," and hangs up, returning to his desk. He glances at Ted, and, once again, they exchange a knowing glance, but no words.

Ted approaches with a portfolio problem and homework sheet in hand, "Do we need anything else copied?" "I don't think so." Ted leaves to do the necessary copying. John looks up and spies a student playfully swatting another with a sponge. "Hey, Nick, what're you doing, buddy?" "Cleaning!"

"I thought so," John replies, monitoring the behavior until it changes.

This is the team's first year in this new space, and the classroom is extremely well-organized. Book shelves hold bankers' boxes neatly labeled with tags such as, "Weekly Reader," "Lake Books," and "Paper." Student desks are in groups of three and four, facing the front of the room.

"Okay. People at the computers, if everyone would sit down please... If you folks would push in your chairs, please," John asks. As students are seated in the desk area, he asks them to straighten their desks and to pick up any small pieces of paper that may be on the floor around them. The students do so without comment, a task to which they clearly are accustomed.

John begins to prepare the students for the transition into math class. "All right, at this time, if you had a math lesson over the weekend, you should have it out. You should be open in the book to that particular lesson. That way, when you go to math class, you'll be all set." Ted returns with the copying in hand and begins to hole-punch the papers. John continues to address the class, praising them for their hard work during the third quarter and encouraging them to keep focused for the final quarter of the year. They pass out the freshly copied assignment sheets. He then dismisses one-third of the class, who exit the room.

Math is the one time during the day when these students are grouped by ability, with Ted, John, and the special educator each taking one section of students. Ted remains in the room with his group, and John takes his into the adjacent, but separate, space next door. Each partner teacher works with his group on fractions, Ted's group with multiplying, and John's with reducing. From time to time, John's voice spills over into the main classroom; yet the students are not distracted by this, accustomed to working with several activities occurring in one space. In fact, this is a great improvement over last year when the three math classes were divided only by thin partitions.

As the math class ends, the students from the other two groups wait quietly at the door until Ted motions them in. They eagerly join Ted's group in their classroom. As the students assemble, Ted directs, "Let's get our assignment sheets out, please."

Before returning to the class, John meets briefly with two boys who had not completed their homework. They fill out "missing homework" sheets, which are letters to parents informing them of any missing assignments. Ted and John send home these letters after the first missing assignment and have noted a significant reduction in the number of late assignments this year, because of, they believe, this new system they implemented.

As John returns, Ted asks him, "Do you want to talk to them about orbital studies?" "Yes," he replies, and the two confer in the front of the room while students put their papers away. Together they then describe orbital studies, a new project to the class, one that entails students' choosing their own topic to research and present to the class during the fourth marking period. Ted initially informs the class, while John extends his ideas and provides examples. "We may have been helping you a bit too much this year. Now we want to help you become more independent with your learning," Ted begins. "Example: We send home a note when your homework isn't in. That's not going to happen in the other grades," John interjects. "It will be up to you to find your own information and make your own decisions about how to present your projects," Ted continues.

"Suggestion: some groups have computer time in the morning. Use that time wisely. Get information from the computer," John offers. Ted perches on the stool in front of the room and elaborates, "In choosing a topic, choose one you don't already know a lot about, but make sure there is information available." "Friday, I think we ought to know what your topic will be," John says with a questioning tone, glancing at Ted. Ted nods and adds, "Even Thursday. That way Friday they can go to the library." "So you need to be thinking about it today," John instructs the class. "And you don't want to choose a topic that's too broad," Ted warns. "Here's an example: the universe. Too broad. But, asteroids, okay," John points out. They continue ⋅vith this pattern of instruction and clarification with the students, describing and exemplifying, elaborating on one another's responses, until it is time for break.

"Okay. Break here?" Ted checks with John. "Yes." The two remain in the front of the room, talking with students who approach them with topic ideas for their independent projects. Eventually, the teachers wind their way over to their desks, and pull out snacks, as most of the students have done by now. As Ted peels an orange, he listens to John's concerns about the pending behavior plan of one of their incoming students, which the special education department is creating for next year. "It would make more sense to me to have a behavior plan just until the end of this year." "Right," Ted agrees, "Different setting, different teachers." They continue this conversation, reflecting on the behavior plans of other students in order to consider what makes an effective plan. "That reminds me," he expands, "we need to look through our conference notes to follow up on suggestions and requests. There was one child we thought we would refer for speech and language. Who was that?" John reminds Ted of who the student is, and they continue to discuss their plans for that until break is over. "Okay. Everybody sit down please," John calls out. The students return to their desks, and he asks them to take out a sheet of paper for spelling words, which, he reminds them, come from the context of the Voyage of the Mimi. The special educator appears in the door, and Ted goes over to consult with her while John continues the class. He writes 15 spelling words on the whiteboard, and the students copy them into their notebooks. Ted returns and circulates the students' desks, helping when necessary. John stumbles over the pronunciation of "bromeliads," and laughs, looking to Ted for assistance. Ted laughs too, supplying the correct pronunciation.

Ted and John go down the list, assisting the students with definitions. When they arrive at a fishing term, Ted turns to John and says, "You want to explain that one to them? Because I don't really understand what it is." Ted reads aloud the dictionary definition, and John takes a couple of minutes to describe in greater detail what purpose a bail on a fishing rod serves. Ted reminds John that one of the student's desks still needs to be repaired. John grabs an Allen wrench from the top drawer of his desk and goes over to fix the desk, while Ted keeps the focus on spelling and vocabulary.

As students work at their desks, Ted and John confer over a binder that contains a unit on Gary Paulson's *Hatchet,* a novel they are to begin today. As they flip the pages of the binder, they refresh one another's memories of what worked last year, and what they want to try this year.

"Okay. Time's up! Please clear your desks! It's time for a review game for Voyage of the Mimi!" John erases the board, and Ted clears papers out of the way. They divide the room in half. Ted draws a tic-tac-toe outline on the board. Ted takes charge of leading this review game, while John grabs Friday's quizzes and works on correcting them. The students enjoy the game, laughing and joking, but also showing some concern for the number of questions they are missing. "It seems from our review that you need to do some studying!" Ted suggests, as he dismisses them for lunch.

Ted and John eat their lunches in the classroom, discussing the day and their plans. After 20 minutes they go to the cafeteria to pick up their students and take them outside for 15 minutes of recess. They stand in the bright April sunshine, bracing themselves against a north wind, watching the students run, play games, and huddle in groups, laughing and talking. The partners discuss their families and the next week's vacation plans.

When recess is over, they return with the students to their classroom, and Ted reads aloud the latest Internet response from a student in a different state, responding to an ongoing book conversation they are holding on the Internet. Then the students take out their books and read silently at desks for the next 15 minutes. John continues to grade the quizzes.

One student raises her hand and asks, "Are we going to get our quizzes back?" John replies, "By the end of the day. You folks are spoiled, usually getting them the same day you take them! You only took this on Friday, you know!" He jokes with them as he hands the graded set to Ted, who records them. As students finish reading, John dismisses them to go to art and music, and the teachers rush off to a meeting with their principal about one of their student's behavior plans. Although this is their one planning period, it is often filled with meetings such as this one.

At the end of the period, students and teachers return to the room, and prepare to begin their new novel, *Hatchet*. John asks the students to line up, and he passes out a copy of the book to each of them. He perches on the stool in front of the room and asks them to analyze the front cover for meaning. They discuss the title and the illustrations before beginning reading aloud. While John leads this activity, Ted gathers homework for an absent student and takes the work down to the office to be picked up.

The final period of the day is Choice Time, during which students sign up for a variety of electives offered by teachers across grade levels in this school. This time, John remains in the room, leading the study on boating safety with a group of ten students, while Ted goes to the school computer lab to direct a course on technology. After this period they return to their shared classroom.

As students return from their exploratory electives, John and Ted divide the stacks of quizzes and pass them back to the students. There is a great deal of talking and laughing as the students load their backpacks and put on their coats. "I got a 95! What'd you get?" "I got a 96!"

As students are dismissed to catch their busses, John and Ted warmly greet a parent as she arrives for her conference. The meeting goes well, as they use student work to demonstrate to the parent her child's progress. They discuss briefly the transition into seventh grade and express their confidence in her child's ability to make this transition effectively. The conference concludes, and they move immediately into discussing the next day's schedule. They review their plans, and Ted plans to remain a little longer working on his computer, while John dons his coat.

"See you tomorrow!" Ted calls "You bet!" John responds, shaking his head with a laugh. •

2

BENEFITS FOR TEACHERS

*The best way to understand teams is to look at
teams themselves. Their own stories reveal their
accomplishments, skills, emotions, and commitment
better than any abstract commentary or logical
presentation.* — Jan Katzenbach and Douglas Smith

Teaming is the proper way to organize a middle school. When
a team functions effectively, the professional payback is
dramatic. The teachers in our study related the myriad benefits
of working collaboratively. In particular, they reported increased
support, enhanced decision making, professional growth through
reflection and risk taking, and an overall enjoyment of teaching as
direct outcomes of their teamwork.

Support

The support these teachers received from one another took many
forms, and the strength of the bond between them was substantial.
One of them, Hope, recounted.

> Teaming has so many good things about it. The
> sharing of information, sharing of time, having
> someone who is there for you in good times and in
> bad, that you are not in it alone, that you've got that
> support if trouble happens to come about.

These teachers knew clearly and without reservation that their teaching partners would be by their sides, both physically and figuratively. In the field of special education, Adams and Cessna (1993) offer the dance metaphor to describe co-teaching, referring to the rhythm or fluid movement that is created when co-teachers collaborate. This metaphor of a dance is useful in envisioning the ways in which partner teachers stepped in for one another effortlessly, picking up where the other left off, in word or in action. The co-teachers' roles switch as situations and needs unfold. Angie and Nancy chose to describe their partnership as a "tag team," a term given to wrestlers who spell each other in the ring during a match. Angie explained the importance of this "tag team" approach when dealing with especially challenging parents.

> In the tag team approach, Nancy and I are able to take over for each other in the same way. If she sees a student needing attention, she'll intervene. We have one particular really stressful parent who comes in here regularly. We take turns dealing with her. We've been doing a lot of switching because you can get really burned out by a parent who needs daily contact.

While Rob did not use the same descriptor as Nancy and Angie to describe the support he received from Ed, the dynamics were the same.

> I have more quiet days than Ed does. If I am having a bad day, I like to be able to kind of sit and gather myself once before the day gets going. Ed is at full speed a lot faster than I am and up earlier. If I am having a tough day, I'll sit at a table and Ed will know that if I am sitting there he should take over and get things started. We take cues from each other as to when to jump in and are sensitive to what's happening with the other person.

Teachers' support for one another extended beyond the classroom to an awareness of support their partner needed in dealing with the challenges of daily life. Lori, for example, appreciated Yvonne's awareness of the other demands in Lori's life and acknowledged that Yvonne did the same for her.

It is nice to have support from someone who knows
you, knows that you have a couple of kids, a husband,
and a dog. And I recognize Yvonne has a mother who
requires attention. It's great to have someone who
understands and cares enough to say, "Hey, why don't
you get a head start on the drive to New Hampshire. I
will take your last study hall." And she does the same
kind of thing for me.

Both Heather and John spoke of their partner's abilities to take
over for a teammate. Heather offered these comments:

There is always support there. And if you are having
an off day, the other person can be there. For instance,
two weeks ago I had a horrible case of laryngitis but
not enough to stay home. So he took over a large
part of the day. I was still there, still able to do some
things. But he took over leadership in my area as well
as his own.

Adams and Cessna (1993) use a second metaphor, the particle
and the stream, that is useful in describing the environment where
real team teaching occurs. Within a "particle and stream" classroom,
the teachers maintain a flow of activities much like a stream, with
the students becoming the particles flowing through it. Within many
classrooms, a student falling out of the flow would disrupt the flow
for the rest of the learners. Within a co-taught classroom, when a
student falls out of the flow, one of the teachers is able to respond to
the student immediately and in context, while the other maintains the
flow for the remainder of the class. Because of the partnership, these
teachers were able to continue the pace of learning, regardless of
interruptions.

When describing the flow of his classroom, Ted offered,

In school, many, many things interrupt your
classroom, from parents coming to drop something
off, phone calls, kids without their work, and always
the need to call a parent right away. And when you are
by yourself, the choice is basically deal with it then
while putting the class on hold for a little bit, or say,
"I can't deal with it right now. I'm teaching a class.
I'll deal with it during a break." When there are two of

you, one person can always continue the class while
the other person answers the phone, talks to a parent,
deals with a behavior problem, or whatever else might
happen. Being able to deal with little problems right
then and there, which is the best time, is a real plus.

Hope underscored Ted's sentiments and extended them by noting
the implicit understanding that developed between Hope and Krista.

It happens a lot more than people think. For instance,
today I had to talk to the superintendent on the phone,
just had to. Krista was able to finish up my last
evaluation and get the kids rolling. I didn't have to
tell her, "Please have those kids assessed and have the
other kids practice." She just knew what needed to be
done.

Almost all of our partner teams used the analogy of a marriage
to describe their working relationships. Although there is still limited
research available exclusively on partner teams, literature on family
and marital theory offers insights into understanding the complex
work of partner teams. As the partner relationship evolves, the
individuals move from explicit talk to implicit understanding (Sillars,
1995), and they are able to communicate with less talk and greater
tacit understanding.

Hope spoke confidently about her faith in their partnership,
explaining how they often covered for one another.

No matter what, Krista covers for me, keeps control of
the class and the integrity of the lesson going. There
is no "I" in team, and you can't be in this business
with an ego. You can't say, "Well, she left me high
and dry." That is never an issue. We always help each
other. It doesn't matter what. It's funny that it happens
so often. Especially with a substitute if you are sick
one day. It's really convenient to have somebody there
who knows the whole picture.

Support, so critical in healthy families, appeared in many forms
within these partner teams.

Decision making

Inherently connected to this ongoing, daily support was a change in decision making that emerged as central to the teaming experiences of these teachers. Because they felt supported and balanced by another well-informed colleague, they perceived themselves making better and more informed decisions. Friend and Cook (1992) name decision making as a central aspect of team teaching; they define collaboration as "a style for direct interaction between at least two co-equal parties voluntarily engaged in shared decision making as they work toward a common goal" (p. 6). For Krista, who previously taught in a self-contained classroom, shared decision making was an incentive to team. For John, formerly a member of a four-person team, making decisions became much easier with only one other person to consult. In fact, it resulted in added flexibility and the ability to expend energy on other needs. He declared:

> We don't have to spend a long time making decisions. That is one of the big advantages of being in a two-teacher team. If we needed to decide on something before, it might take 40 minutes. But now it might take seconds. With a team of four other teachers, you have to have a meeting that takes so much time and energy. Now our energy can be spent on other things.

Ed described a similar experience.

> Most of my experience had been on four- and five-person teams. It was a relief to be able to make small moves quickly. Rob and I can come to a decision sometimes turning on a dime. With a five-person team, first of all you've got to get them all around the table at the same time. Reaching consensus isn't easy especially with the teachers who have been at this quite awhile. They have their differences and opinions. With two people we still might disagree, but it's quicker to work it out.

The partners on these teams tended to reflect on their prior teaming experiences as a way to illustrate the attributes and outcomes of their present partner team. They often referred to previous interdisciplinary teams as falling short of "true" teaming and depicted the larger team as a place where the struggle for consensus predominated. Making decisions was a primary cause of frustration on large teams. The partner unit provided the support, creativity, and critical questioning of working with others, yet reduced the struggle for consensus and the limited access to flexibility and spontaneity.

These teams also identified the lack of attention to joint decision making as the stimulus for anger or disagreement. When asked what kinds of events spurred moments when they experienced disagreement, Krista answered quickly, "Decisions one of us made autonomously and then tried to check with the other after the fact." With mutual decision making as a norm in the partnership, when one of the partners strayed from this norm it became a point of contention. Just as consistent, internal norms contribute to the health of a family, so do they also contribute to the effectiveness of the partner team relationship.

Professional growth

In describing outcomes of their experiences, these teachers identified partner teaming as an important avenue for professional growth. Heather speculated, "I think growing professionally is a biggie, the way that we have grown together. I don't know if I would have gotten so far as an individual teacher." A novice teacher when their teaming began, Hope reflected on the powerful learnings her partner offered her.

> I have faith that what Krista does is really good
> for kids, and the way that she approaches meeting
> children's needs, and the way she is passionate about
> getting the right thing for that kid at the moment...
> her timing in a lesson is incredible.... How to look at
> a huge unit and break it down into reasonable chunks.
> Those are things that I'm sure that I might have come
> to realize on my own, but it would have taken me a lot
> longer than it did.

Hope's reflection on her professional growth resonates strongly with the broader literature on teacher collaboration. There is a clear relationship between teacher collaboration and increased feelings of teacher efficacy (Johnson, 1990; Rosenholtz, 1985). Within a continuum of teacher-collegial relations, Little (1990) describes joint work, the deepest stage of collaboration on the continuum, as a form of partnering where teachers engage in team teaching, planning, and sustained peer coaching.

Hope continued by explaining how her academic expertise had been broadened.

> What teaming opens up is the opportunity to share your information. And so often we focus on a content area; we don't want to give it up because that is our expertise. But when we give that up and take something else on and seek that balance, we are really expanding ourselves. I know I'm a better teacher as a result of this teaming experience. I know so much more about literature and math now that I never would have experienced had I been in my own little seventh-grade classroom just teaching science.

Krista shared this perspective, and discussed advantages of questioning her partner's practices and ideas in a healthy manner.

> We think the same way in so many ways—philosophy, theory. But when we differ, whatever comes out is so much better. When she says, "I think we should teach it this way," and I say, "No, I think this way is better," we get into a really good discussion. Whatever comes out of that is really great. It's wonderful.

Reflection

Critical questioning is one characteristic of a truly collaborative culture, as Little (1990) described such cultures as joining "colleagues and their expertise together to generate critical yet also practically grounded reflection on what they do as a basis for wiser, more skilled action" (p. 515). In questioning each other's practice, partners moved toward refining their vision of what it means to work with students in a developmentally responsive manner, and grew professionally through that refinement.

For example, Nancy valued the fact that Angie would ask her to pause and take time to look at an issue.

> If Angie feels very strongly about something, I will usually support that unquestioningly. On the other

hand, if she knows there is an issue with kids or
families in school that I am very committed to and
feel passionate about, that will be her position too
unless she needs to point out to me or I need to point
out to her why it might not be the best approach. She
might say, "Let me just share with you why I think
this isn't going to work." We do that in a way that still
maintains the integrity of our partnership. It doesn't
compromise in any way, but it permits us to look at
things differently and critically.

Sarah felt that it was vital for teammates to challenge each other
to ensure they were growing and evolving as a team in positive,
effective ways and also taking time to be reflective. We are always
asking ourselves, "What did you think when this happened? or What
do you think about the way this went?"

Erica's and Shannon's level of comfort in challenging one
another was obviously a visible part of their relationship. One
seventh-grade student described this part of his teachers' relationship:

It's like if one gets out of line, she will pull the other
one into the office and say "You better settle down,
you are getting a little out of control here." They help
each other. They warn each other when one thinks the
other is off the edge. I guess they do this because they
are best friends. They have worked together, forever.

The close relationship that developed between the two partners
allowed them to support and challenge one another. The level of trust
and respect present within partner teams provided a safe foundation
that allowed the teachers to feel secure in challenging and being
challenged. Without this foundation, the questioning of another's
teaching practices could be intimidating and threatening to one's
professional competence. The teachers' willingness to challenge
one another stimulated their professional growth and encouraged
reflection about their teaching practices. While teachers' pedagogical
practices obviously benefited from this willingness to question one
another, the students were, of course, the ultimate winners. Their
learning needs were explicitly examined as a result of the teachers'
willingness to engage in dialogue. Reflection played a critical role
for teachers as they revisited and revised their practices.

Erica and Shannon provided a strong example of ongoing reflection. They commute to school together, not only for the added planning time it allows them, but also for the reflective time it afforded. Yet, for this team, reflection did not end when the car ride did. On the contrary, these two slipped naturally and readily into a reflective mode during the day, walking down the hallway, at lunch or break time, any moment they had. As they walked to lunch, they began to surmise about two of their students who "just don't seem to learn the way we are teaching." They pondered this dilemma, exploring what had worked for them, and what had not.

Ted and John also demonstrated the reflective nature of their work as they took a moment during break time to discuss a child who will enter their class in the fall. The administration was encouraging them to set up a behavior plan for this child. They were opposed, feeling that a different setting and different teachers would have a different effect on the child, and that they would need time with this student to observe his or her nature and needs. They spent the remainder of the break discussing another child with a current behavior plan, and what had worked and not worked for that student this year. Ted and John also used time in the summer to revisit the successes and failures of the previous school year, adjusting their plans based on these reflections.

The increased perspective about their work that the teachers experienced when working together also nurtured their professional growth. Shannon explained this in terms of what she saw as safeguarding objectivity.

> I think it is good to have two viewpoints. There have been times when I've said, "We need to do this." And Erica has said "Hold on." Or vice versa... I do think that having another person's view is important to maintain objectivity.

Erica discussed the value of an additional point of view in providing insight into their students and pointed out that the special educator on the team provided a third set of eyes when observing students and their behaviors.

Taking risks

The support to take risks also enabled these teachers to grow professionally and personally. Krista explained, "We have been willing to make a leap and know that we will come out of it okay if we stick together." Nancy described the changes in her general attitude about school as a result of her partnership with Angie. "My first five years here, I was inflexible, rigid, didn't try new things. But this teaming relationship has made me more relaxed. I've experienced a lot more joy in what I do every day and am more willing to try various things."

Having confidence in each other was the key for Sarah and Betsy when they wanted to try a new approach in their teaching.

> Having confidence that we can do it, confidence in each other, confidence that it will work out. Like this year when we were teaching math for the first time and thought, "We can't have every kid in a heterogeneous group on the same page for computation. They are all in different places. How are we going to do this?" And so we tried letting the kids choose which page they needed to work on. We just made up the plan with a way to keep a record. Maybe it wouldn't work, but there is something about our confidence; so we just went ahead.

As Krista described her relationship with other teachers in their building, she stressed the support Hope provided as they took the risk to lead professional development for others.

> We've been on the outs with the staff at different times because we often are seen as starting new things and then being asked to explain it to the staff who look at us and say to themselves, "Oh, there are Hope and Krista again doing their stuff." I wouldn't have the guts to teach the faculty unless Hope were a partner. Together I feel strong, whereas separately, I don't think I would.

Shannon's words highlighted the power of two people working together, as she detailed a time when she felt physically safe to take a risk because of Erica's support.

In our first year teaming we had a seventh-grader
who we were certain was being abused at home. But
we had no proof. When she got a bad report card she
was scared to go home. So we decided that we were
going to the trailer where her father was so we could
talk with him about her report card before he lit into
her and try to avert the kid's getting beaten. When
we showed up, her abusive father was loaded. As
an individual I would not have put myself in danger
going there. There is safety in numbers.

This concept of safety, physical or emotional, was central to the
degree of risk these partners felt they might take. The support they
received from being in close partnership enabled them to stretch
themselves to go beyond their usual performance. If a particular
approach did not work, teachers on these partner teams would try
something else without hesitation. Their willingness to take chances
and try things from a new perspective enriched their teaching
strategies.

Enjoyment of teaching

Reflecting on the teaming experience, Hope said simply,
"Teaching can be a really lonely profession when you work by
yourself." These teachers we studied expressed the extreme
satisfaction and enjoyment they received from teaching and how that
related to partner teaming. Ted explained that adult companionship
unquestionably enhanced his teaching experience.

The idea of having someone to share with makes so
much sense. If there were no adult companionship all
day, just with the kids all day and not able to share
experiences with an adult, teaching wouldn't be nearly
as much fun.

Hope shared that sentiment, as she explained how working with
Krista provided her with an incentive to go beyond her usual level
of activity. "I enjoy coming to work and seeing that familiar face
with a greeting like… We have sugar doughnuts today. That kind of
interaction makes me want to do more." Hope reported she enjoyed
talking about everyday events. There was a tone of mutual and
reciprocal affirmation in these teachers' voices. Their enjoyment of

teaching and the satisfaction in the work they do parallel the findings of satisfied married couples who have been found to spend more time talking with one another than those less satisfied (Sillars, 1995). The literature also points out feelings of personal isolation for teachers on teams, diminishing to non-existent by early in the school year (see Mills, Powell, & Pollack, 1992).

Nancy summarized the value of working on a partner team and the difference it made in her outlook both about teaching and about her students.

> Before I began working on this team with Angie, I was lonely. I mean, really lonely. The only contact I had with other adults was between classes. Now teaching is exciting. When people ask, "What do you teach?" I respond positively that I teach a five/six multiage team with a partner. They usually say, "Well, that must be really hard." But I retort, "No, every day is different. It's challenging." Everything is shaped by kids and what Angie and I decide to do; it's constantly changing. But more than anything I guess, even though I know it doesn't sound very lofty, it's just fun. It really is.

Overall, these partner team teachers voiced important outcomes of their collaboration. They attributed support, professional growth, enhanced decision making, and an overall enjoyment of teaching as direct results of their collaborative work. For teachers on effective partner teams, the payoff is great. Nancy's feeling that her job was "fun and joyful" translated into a classroom with similar attributes. We explore this and other outcomes for students in Chapter 3. ⑥

HEATHER AND ALAN

It is a rainy, end-of-the-year Friday. Alan and Heather both arrive early and chat with one another about their respective families. Friday is Sneaker Day for their sixth-grade team, and they both sport sneakers with their otherwise professional dress. Their wide, double classroom is filled with student work on walls and books; folders and boxes are piled high on the shelves along the wall, the accumulation of years of teaching. Each side of the room boasts a poster-sized photograph of the team of students and teachers. There are four computers on desks against each of the far walls. There is also a telephone on Alan's side of the room. Large, wooden rolling doors replaced a center wall four years ago at Heather and Alan's request and enable the teachers to open and close the two rooms at their convenience. These doors are open to start the day.

"How did Ryan's baseball game go last night?" Heather inquires about Alan's son's performance as she sorts papers on her desk. Their families know one another well, at times dining or attending sporting events together. In the small town, the local sports teams bring a sense of community to the residents, and Heather and Alan are not exceptions to this feeling. The fact that they each live within two miles of the school increases the ease of their involvement with all school activities.

"Oh, it went well! He went three for four!" Alan replies enthusiastically. They easily move from social conversation into business. Sitting at a round table on Heather's side of the room, they review plans for the day. Heather reminds Alan that the students need more time to work on their skits for the DARE graduation exercises. As they plan their schedule for the days ahead, the conversation is a gradual building on each other's suggestions and reminders. Out of it they start to paint a picture of the days to come. Students begin to arrive, their ready laughter and chatter permeating the air. Alan and Heather greet them with smiles, and the teachers disperse to their individual sides of the room. The 32 students on this team are often divided into two groups of 16 for more effective instruction and assessment. These "blue" and "gold" sections, named after the school colors, are heterogeneous.

The students clearly know the morning routine; they pick up their journals on the way to their desks, preparing for the usual, five-minute journal-write that starts the day. Heather reminds a few laggards to retrieve their journals. Holding a stopwatch in her hand. "Five, four, three, two, one!" she counts down, pressing her thumb on the top button. The students' pens are off and running, scribbling furiously in their notebooks.

After the journal-write, Heather and Alan take lunch count, and then the students are free to use the remaining homeroom time to complete assignments, individual or group projects, or make-up work. Several students read; two boys work at their desks writing end-of-the-year reflections; a group of girls practices a skit, glancing around self-consciously from time to time; and five boys work in the back of the room, crafting a five-foot, cardboard rocket for the survival unit.

As homeroom comes to a close, Heather pulls the walls shut to begin language arts, while Alan directs mathematics activities with the other half of the class. "Okay. Let's get your reading journals," Heather announces. The students rise to get their journals. They write in them at their desks, reflecting on a variety of themes: what has happened most recently in their books, the actions of the main characters, and the connections between the books and personal experience. Heather circulates, pausing to provide writing ideas to those students who are stuck in pencil chewing mode. "Why don't you try predicting what's going to happen next in your book?" Heather suggests, "Use the title to help you."

As students finish, Heather reminds them that class today will ⟩rimarily consist of workshop time. Often, workshop time is used to hold peer conferences or book presentations. Today, it is set aside to enable the students to work independently or in small groups on work that is due. Heather moves toward the table in the back of her room and reaches for her status-of-the-class chart. She checks with students to see where they are in their books or to record the titles of new books just begun. She also uses the time to touch base with students who are missing work. "Nicole, you did not get your health report into me yesterday," she reminds gently, but sternly. "Oh yeah!" A girl in a purple tee-shirt jumps up smiling to retrieve the missing item.

During workshop time, students use the time on a variety of assignments; most are busy composing their end-of-the-year reflections in which they discuss relevant learnings from the course of the school year. Heather responds to several questions about the assignment, circulating aournd the room, ensuring that all students are on task. Her manner is businesslike, yet gentle. A few students come and go freely to use the bathroom in the hall, taking the wooden pass as they go. As they finish one task, Heather identifies several others for them to work on—reading responses, reading contracts, spell checking, reading independently. The atmosphere is busy and work-centered, and Heather momentarily scoots next door to confer with Alan about the time he needs to finish the math lesson.

As the time draws to a close, Heather addresses the whole class, "Okay, you've got about five minutes left. As you're finishing up, I'd like Rosa and Mikayla to turn in their journals today. All of you, don't forget, your books should be finished by next Friday, and your response is due Tuesday."

The students put their work away, and Heather reads aloud from *The Plant That Ate Dirty Socks*, beginning by asking some students to summarize what happened last time. As she reads, she pauses from time to time to make connections between the book and the students' lives. "Do any of your closets look like that?" She jokes with them as a passage about the protagonist's lack of tidiness is read. Heather reads standing up, pacing back and forth as the story progresses, adding body language to her expressive reading.

As the time slips away, one boy requests, "Can I see if they're ready?" He is referring to the other half of their team. Heather nods, and he darts out the door into the hallway and pokes his head into Alan's half of the classroom. Alan gives him a thumbs-up, and he returns with the message. The students slide the walls open between the rooms, and the groups switch places.

Alan slides the walls back into place, chats with the new group of students about the recent success of the girls' sports team, and begins class. "Okay. Get your homework out, please, and trade math papers with your neighbor." They correct their homework as Alan calls the answers aloud and writes on the overhead projector. He moves quickly, informing the class that they have a lot to do today. The students follow along, assessing their peers' papers as he goes. In the middle of this process, the telephone rings, and Alan answers.

As the head teacher in the building, Alan fills the role of disciplinarian while the principal is away. He asks the Chapter One teacher to cover for him, and she picks up where he left off as he strolls out of the room. Alan returns moments later, followed by a student who had been wandering the halls. Alan points to a desk near the front of the room; the student sits there and works on math homework. A few moments later, Heather arrives and confers with Alan about her student, and they decide to let him remain where he is. Alan proceeds with his class. Students exchange papers, sometimes exclaiming over their scores, and Alan collects the homework.

The atmosphere is warm and friendly, and the students seem comfortable joking and chatting with Alan and one another. He leads them through several examples of the division of fractions, and then directs them to problems for more practice. As the students begin, Alan returns to the student in the front of the room and suggests he work on a variety of assignments due to Heather. Because of their close teaming arrangement, Alan knows what work is being accomplished on the other side of the wall.

At 10:00 Alan asks his students to finish up with mathematics, and he shifts into social studies where they have been learning about the U.S. Constitution. Students discuss the rights the Constitution provides, including the right to bear arms and how this impacts their community.

As they finish, Alan and Heather open the sliding walls together. Alan announces, "Those of you who are eligible for break may go to snack. If you owe work, wait here patiently." Many students jump up to get in line; a few stay at their desks. Alan goes outside with the students, and Heather remains inside with those who need to complete work.

Because it is Friday, the students move from break to physical education or music class. This provides Heather and Alan their one full planning period each week. First, they each take approximately 10 minutes to deal with individual issues. Today, Heather works on the student-of-the-week board, and Alan, as chief negotiator for the local teachers' union, deals with a pressing negotiation matter. When these tasks are completed, the two meet at a group of students' desks in between their two classroom spaces. Because this is the only scheduled planning meeting within the school day each week, these two partners meet regularly and often in the evenings and on weekends at school and at their homes. It is during these post-school hours when most of the long-range planning occurs. They devote this Friday meeting mostly to day-to-day procedural matters.

Alan with his grade book in hand and Heather with a pile of manila folders begin the meeting by compiling an agenda from a collection of notes that Heather has collected over the week. As they settle into their meeting, Heather remembers that today is a student's birthday. Alan moves over to the computer and quickly creates a birthday card. Heather informs him that she will create the permission slip for the end-of-the-year pool party, and together they brainstorm what needs to be on it. During the course of their meeting, the guidance counselor and the special educator arrive at different times to discuss certain students. Heather and Alan easily fit these conversations in and then return to their team planning.

"Okay, let's do the student-of-the-week," Heather directs. They review their grade books for the blue and gold sections. "What about Jessie Stevens?" Alan suggests. "Great idea!" Heather responds, and she shares an anecdote about a powerful journal entry Jessie wrote this week. They move on to discussing the report card schedule. "I'm going to have my grades done soon; guess I'd better make up the list." Alan reports with a laugh, "No, I'll type it up for you," Heather is quick to offer. "I need to learn to make the template better, so I'll do it." Alan assumes ownership of this task. Together they compose a list of assignments that belong on the rank card.

"Now we need to decide on percentages for the weighting of assignments," Heather states. "I'll do that," Alan offers. "And I'll do all of the science grading," Heather adds. They move on to rearranging their schedule for next week; Heather relies on Alan's skills to redistribute the times evenly.

This back and forth of task assignments is swift and appears effortless. It occurs naturally between the partners, with one of them identifying a need, and the two of them determining how best to fill it. As tasks arise, they use their strengths to assign them. This process continues throughout the meeting as they discuss the schedule for the rest of the day and for next week. They build on the other's ideas, finishing the other's sentences, agreeing, and praising the other for good ideas.

When the students return, Alan announces, "Okay, have a seat, please." Their teachers each hold up two fingers as a signal for silence. The partners stand by the open, sliding doors, addressing the whole team.

"Okay, we need your attention," Heather states. "Today you'll have 45 minutes to work on your survival unit project. Time is running out; it's due next Friday. We have other things to get done, and Mr. C is going to talk about that. Think about the time you have left and what you need to do."

"How much time do we have today?" one student asks. "45 minutes," Alan repeats for him. "But first we're going to give you a few minutes today to establish groups for your DARE skits. You'll have 25 minutes to determine who's in your group, to assign parts, and write one or two sentences about your skit." "Can we have partners from both blue and gold?" another student asks. In unison the teachers nod their heads affirmatively. The students busy themselves getting into groups, and the two teachers circulate throughout both sides of the room, pausing at groups to ask who the recorder for the group is and answering a variety of questions. The students work in their groups brainstorming, laughing as they work.

After collecting the recorder's notes from the skit, Alan continues to circulate. Heather gathers some props for next week's open house and dashes out to photocopy an assignment for a student. Alan addresses the class, "We need to move on, so take the next two minutes to assign tasks. Then work in your survival groups until lunch." Heather returns, and the two confer about an absent student and how to incorporate her into a skit. The students busy themselves with their survival projects, bringing out dioramas, board games, posters, and other creations to use in their presentations next week. Heather and Alan circulate, assisting in design ideas, refilling rubber cement jars, and providing moral support to the group whose cardboard rocket refuses to stand. The time passes quickly, and soon they inform students that it is time to pick up and go to lunch.

Heather and Alan follow their students into the cafeteria and check to see that the lunch line moves swiftly and orderly, then they grab their lunches and join five other teachers at a round table in the middle of the cafeteria where they keep their eyes on the room around them. The conversation around the lunch table centers on local school sports. Several of the teachers are parents of high school athletes, and this community connection beyond the workplace lends an element of ease to their rapport. As head teacher, Alan is pulled from the conversation from time to time to deal with student issues. Lunch time lasts 20 minutes, followed by 10 minutes of recess. The teachers return to their rooms to prepare for the students' return.

Continuing with the survival unit, Heather and Alan offer mini-courses in the afternoon. Heather works with half of the students in the gymnasium, training them in CPR. Alan works outside with the other half on orienteering and fire building. These groups switched halfway through the unit so all students could learn all of the skills. When they finish with the mini-courses, the team returns to the double classroom. As the students sit in homeroom groups, their teachers remind them of homework. Heather and Alan excuse the team by busload until eventually they are the only ones remaining. They straighten their desks, gathering up what they will need that evening, and head to a health curriculum committee meeting, chatting about the double header baseball and softball games they hope to attend later this afternoon. •

3

BENEFITS FOR STUDENTS

*In any situation requiring the real time combination
of multiple skills, experiences, and judgments, a team
inevitably gets better results than a collection of
individuals operating within confined job roles and
responsibilities.* — Katzenbach and Smith

Eleven percent of teachers in the United States resign after just
one year teaching, 21 percent after two years, and 39 percent
after five years (Britton, 2002). These disheartening figures
illustrate the importance of any educational practice that would
support teachers positively and lead to their continuing service.
But since the central purpose of education is student learning, the
question, *Does partner teaming benefit students' learning and
development?* is of primary concern. This chapter will provide an
answer.

Since the onset of the middle school movement, the focus on
creating small communities of learning has echoed in the larger
school restructuring effort (National Middle School Association,
1982; Lounsbury & Vars, 1978; George & Lounsbury, 2000;
Klonskey, 2002; Vander Ark, 2002). The partner team is a small
learning community at its best. Students in such teams benefit in two
main categories: belonging and learning.

Belonging

At the most fundamental level, teaming addresses the adolescent's need to belong to a meaningful group, breaking down feelings of isolation and anonymity and enabling him or her to develop academically and personally (Arhar, 1994; Epstein, 1981). These feelings of belonging contribute significantly to students' readiness to learn. The adolescent's need to belong is well-documented in literature. For instance, Stevenson (2002) says, "Being affiliated with something good seems to be a part of every youngster's self-description. Whether it is a sports team, or an informal group, or one's family, kids talk about themselves in terms of their affiliation…" (p.86). When students lack a sense of belonging to their school or family, they are likely to seek it somewhere, all too often by joining a gang. The vast majority of gang members are reported to be from 15 to 24 years of age (Office of Juvenile Justice and Delinquency Prevention, 1999), highlighting the importance of reaching students during their middle grades years and building healthy affiliations. While gang activity is most prevalent in large cities, it is now found in suburban areas and small towns. Position papers and policy documents guiding middle level education universally assert the importance of building affiliation through teaming. "Creating teams of teachers and students is a vital part of developing a middle grades learning community" (Jackson & Davis, 2000, p.125). Partner teams magnify the advantages of teaming in many ways (Allen-Malley & Bishop, 2000; Bishop & Stevenson, 2000). By having approximately half as many students as a four-teacher team and having these fewer students twice as long, the partner team achieves a fundamental gain in the student-teacher ratio that leads to other advantages.

How do effective partner team teachers characterize their relationships with students? How do they describe their approaches to building affiliation on teams? And how do their students describe their feelings about the teams? As illustrated through the vignettes in this book, the two-teacher teams presented here consist of between 30 and 60 students per team who spend at least half of their day with two teachers in shared or adjacent classrooms. During this concentrated time together meaningful relationships between teachers and students are forged.

All of the teachers talked about creating a sense of belonging and acceptance on their teams. However, Angie's metaphor of the team as family was particularly powerful in capturing the feeling the teachers wanted to create on their team.

> We talk about the concept of family a lot. I think the kids see that there are different ways to look at family and that we have some of the same relationships here. What has been most heartening for us is seeing kids stick up for each other in the way they would stick up for others in their families. The transfer of that concept of family is very important to us and also reminds us how important it is to keep those connections with the kids' out-of-school families.

A sixth grader on Nancy and Angie's team acknowledged her teachers' efforts in creating a sense of family on their team. "You really belong to your classroom and family. And you have like best friends. You've got two families—at your house and at school."

By working hard to really know and understand their students, Rob felt that he and Ed created a sense of ownership and belonging that included all team members, teachers and students alike. "With the two-teacher team knowing the kids so well we always come back to the idea that we are in this together. It is not a *you* versus *me* thing; it's an *us* together."

A seventh-grade student on Rob and Ed's team agreed with her teachers' analysis of how their team worked. "It's like one big family. We don't leave some people out. If we are doing a class activity, we want everybody to be a part of it."

Ensuring that group identity continued to be part of the team's culture required constant monitoring. Nancy explained that the process of building a sense of team identity or family was something that evolved over time.

> Our students understand what we are doing and why we are doing it. It's not like we throw them to this wolf den of 47 other kids. Everything in here is purposeful. It is essential for the kids to see that. We even say to them sometimes, 'Do you know why we are doing this?' And if you get those blank looks, then we stop; for we are not ready to move ahead yet.

While the teachers on these teams are still clearly in charge, the traditional hierarchical and often adversarial relationship between teacher and students is replaced with a more collaborative and cooperative one. The references to the team as a "we" reflected an environment of mutual responsibility and constant give and take throughout the school day. The teachers foster this culture through efforts to get to know the students on a more personal level—and the reverse was true as well. On these effective partner teams, personal knowledge of one another eroded the stereotypes and misconceptions that support a more traditional autocratic classroom.

The strong relationships forged on these two-teacher teams led students and teachers alike to universally characterize the team as "family." This powerful metaphor succinctly captures the relationships that developed between the teachers and students.

On these partner teams respect was the norm guiding the daily interactions between teachers and between teachers and students. The teachers interacted with each other not unlike loving and respectful parents who strive to provide a supportive and caring environment for their children. Day in and day out, students saw their two teachers working collaboratively. The teachers dealt respectfully with their successes, failures, and conflicts with each other in their efforts to provide students with a supportive and caring learning environment.

For some students, the interactions between the two teachers provided perhaps their only exposure to a balanced, healthy relationship and a culture of respect. The influence of their positive modeling on young adolescents, who are making both conscious and unconscious decisions about how they will act as adults, cannot be underestimated. This modeling provides an important counterbalance to the often violent and disrespectful interactions many students see in the media and occasionally in their homes.

The teachers were aware of the benefits for students their teaming offered. Ted recounted,

> It helps the kids see us get along well. We ask them to work together a lot, and they see us working together and having fun doing it. They watch us teaming all day long. They usually participate. I think probably this meant more to them than all the talking about how to work with a teammate that we did.

Family systems' theory illuminates the powerful role that members of the "family" exert upon one another. Briefly stated, the actions of individuals have the power to impact the functionality of a family. Children's behavior is influenced by their developmental attitudes, living conditions, interactions with others, and the values, attitudes, and beliefs of their family of origin (Stanberry, 1994). If the family-like nature of these teams exerts a small portion of the influence that family systems' theory suggests, the role of modeling in partner teaming is significant indeed. These teachers share the perspective that, through their ongoing interactions with their partners, they demonstrate to students the skills of working collaboratively and of balancing work and play in life.

Baumrind's (1991) compelling research on parenting also helps to illustrate the similarity between a parenting relationship and the relationship and commitment on the part of the two teachers toward their students. For example, authoritative parenting is supportive and responsive to a child's needs while at the same time setting standards with high expectations. Students who grow up in families with an authoritative parenting style have "better psychosocial development, school grades, greater self reliance, and lower levels of delinquent behavior" (p.53). Partner teams can provide a similar authoritative structure. These partner teams set standards of behavior based on respect, which all students observe. The teachers provide students with consistency and predictability in their academic program as well as in their interpersonal relationships. They also provide the support and sense of belonging that make students feel safe and accepted and help them gain the confidence to take risks in their learning. As Betsy asserted, "We work to provide them with chances to be successful. We know what they can do, and we create options for them to do it so they can experience success." The teachers' dedication to providing a structure that allowed each student to realize her or his full potential is strikingly similar to parents' devotion to their children.

The family metaphor extends to the pride students felt as members of their team. A sense of pride about team affiliation existed on all the teams we studied, although with varying degrees of intensity. While some students expressed disappointment with the small amount of time they spent with friends on other teams, they still felt that the best place to be was on their team. This echoes many of the feelings of young adolescents about their affiliations with their own family and with their peer group. While they are often reluctant to publicly acknowledge any association with their family, especially their parents, it is still important for them to know their parents are available and accessible when needed.

This culture of team as "family" goes well beyond many of the policy recommendations that provide all students with a small, caring group of adults. The teachers' efforts to create and sustain a family-like environment provide students with a sense of security, acceptance, safety, and, in some cases, love. Some might argue that the teachers' efforts to create this environment violate the boundaries between home and school. However, the teachers reported that, for some children, the school environment was their only experience of a stable, predictable, and loving family situation.

How do teachers achieve this sense of community and family? When asked to describe their strategies for building this affiliation for young adolescents, teachers identified two concepts as critical: caring and respect.

Caring for students. Rob said, "I think it is essential that the teachers really love middle level kids. If they don't get along with or really like this age group, they will never survive. These kids need and demand so much of you. It's an intense and often exhausting, but exhilarating experience." The students were keenly aware that their teachers cared about them and genuinely wanted to know them as individuals. One seventh-grade student in Erica and Shannon's class described his perceptions about his teachers' concern for them:

> They ask you questions. They do pry a little bit
> because they want to know you personally. A lot of
> times they will ask us what we did over the weekend
> and how was our weekend. They are almost like more
> than teachers. I mean, they actually care about us. And
> they want to know how we are doing.

That this student characterizes such caring as being "almost like more than teachers" suggests his previous understanding of a teacher's role as one who would not engage in this level of relationship.

An eighth-grader on Rob and Ed's team explained his experience in relation to his earlier experience on a larger, interdisciplinary team.

> It seems like they care a lot more about you because like with four teachers they basically care about the whole group, but with just two teachers you get to know them better. You get a little bit more of one on one. They make it a lot more personal.

Lori explained one downside of making it "a lot more personal," as the student suggested. She described her frustration when they were unable to get additional assistance for their students. Their intimate knowledge of students' needs made them keenly aware of the ramifications of any delay in intervention.

> We go to meeting after meeting, really advocating for these kids. "When is something going to be done? Why isn't this being done?" Not that we didn't do some of this on a five-member team, but because we have them for two years we know them a lot better.

After developing such close relationships, Lori pointed out that saying goodbye to their students is difficult. Yvonne described, "We get very connected to them. This is the hardest time of the year. After being with them for two years, it hurts to let them go."

The care that Nancy and Angie gave their students also resulted in meaningful and long-lasting relationships. Angie explained their ongoing association with their students long after they leave middle school.

> We still have quite a bit of contact. They can't wait to come back to do something here. One of our kids will bring messages from former students about what they are doing. When they are on exam breaks, we get flooded with phone calls. "Can I come back?" They want to be part of a team and help us.

Because students and teachers on these partner teams spend most of their day together in fairly intense contact, they genuinely come to like one another, increasing the chances that the team will function smoothly and effectively. The teachers' explicit efforts to get to know each of the students on a personal level indicate their awareness of this basic requirement. In return, allowing students to get to know them as individuals also is an important part of what made these relationships work. Though each team went about establishing relationships with students in different ways, such efforts were integral to every team's program. As a result, students viewed their teachers as people who were accessible, willing to make time for them, and who genuinely cared about their well-being. Not surprisingly, this focus on caring is highly consistent with the original tenets of the middle school concept.

Partner teams are humane centers of education able to implement so much of what the middle school concept advocates. Particularly striking was the impact the partnership had on these teachers' relationships with at-risk students. In an era in which 25 percent of all 14-year-olds engage in risky behavior, including drinking alcohol, smoking marijuana regularly, and frequently having unprotected intercourse (Dryfoos, 1998), we increasingly ask schools to provide intervention and understanding in a crisis. The partner team organization at the middle level responds to these conditions with two teachers who are able to know young adolescents and be responsible for their needs.

For students, dealing with only two adults both of whom respond in a predictable manner creates a level of safety and security that for some students exists no other place. Angie explained, "The consistency that they see between Nancy and me is really comforting for them. They see that adults can work together, say what they mean and mean what they say; and this condition makes their world safer."

When asked about a time when their teaming played a critical role, Shannon shared a story of one girl about whom they were concerned. The student was struggling with her relationships at home, and that stress carried over into her schoolwork. Shannon's words further illustrated the possibilities for intervention with "at-risk" students.

> The kid came in to take her exam... and walked in
> late, and she and Erica got into it over her being late...I
> think she told the child to leave. But I grabbed her on
> the way out and I asked, "What's going on?" Well,
> the kid had slept in the street the night before. She
> had had real problems with her parents and ended up

sleeping in a stairway. Her life was falling apart. So
I sat her down at the desk and sort of explained to
Erica who had been distracted by five other kids who
were having various problems, and when Erica found
out the circumstances she gave the student the test.
Afterwards Erica said to me, "Thanks, I wouldn't have
known what was going on with that kid if you hadn't
done that."

The role Shannon played in one child's life as a result of her
partnership with Erica is characterized by an ethic of caring. The
ability to be responsive to students and their needs in an individual
manner exemplifies a structure that "encourages the growth of
competent, caring, loving, and lovable people" (Noddings, 1992, p.
xiv).

Over the years middle level literature has been filled with ideas
about the importance of every student's being well known by at
least one adult in the school. The Carnegie Corporation (1995),
for example, provided a strong rationale for establishing teacher
advisories as part of every middle school student's daily school
experience, asserting that every student needs at least one thoughtful
adult who takes the time to talk with the student about academic and
personal problems and the importance of performing well in school.
National Middle School Association's (2003) position paper, *This
We Believe: Successful Schools for Young Adolescents* has as one of
its 14 characteristics, "An adult advocate for every student" (p. 16).
Currently, where they exist, the traditional teacher advisory model
assigns teachers to a group of 10 to 20 students with whom they meet
on a regular basis. Meeting times range widely. Some might meet
every day for 20 minutes; others may meet only three times a week
for 15 minutes, others even less frequently. The time is intended
to be spent connecting socially and academically and enables the
adult to serve as an advocate for those students. Ideally, the advisory
ensures that no child slips through the cracks.

In most cases, the teacher advisory arrangement relies heavily
on the individual advisor's commitment to maintain contact with
advisees' teachers and parents. The effectiveness of advisory
programs has been questioned by many. Effective advisory programs
have been difficult to establish and maintain because of the
challenges of large group size, inadequate administrative support,

and insufficient professional development for advisors (Bunte, 1995; Connors, 1986; Van Hoose, 1991).

Strikingly, most of the partner teams in our study achieved the goals of teacher advocacy as a natural part of the students' day, without the need for a formal program. This occurred because of the teachers' strong emphasis on knowing their students personally and academically, their efforts to create a family-like atmosphere together, their extended time together, and, finally through their strong commitment to regular parent communication. The emotional and academic support for the students was integral to the team's organization and not reliant upon the individual commitment of a single advisor. In partner teams, the objectives of teacher advisory were subsumed in the prevailing conditions. The partner team provides a new and important way of thinking about how the benefits of advisory can be made available to every middle school student.

Developing a culture of respect. Connected to the caring inherent in these partner teams, effective teams require a culture in which all team members, as well as their ideas and property, are equally valued and respected. Teachers on these teams identified this as a necessary component in their relationships with students as they built a sense of affiliation on the team.

Nancy and Angie tried to establish a culture in their classroom that would extend beyond the school walls. By learning to interact respectfully with one another on the team, they felt they positively influenced students' interactions outside the classroom.

> We strive for a better way to do things. We teach the skills necessary for our students to solve their conflicts peacefully, and we expect our students to use those skills. We teach and model respect for all of the things that enable us to be here together, the school property, the faculty and staff, and our families... Usually 25 percent of our class each year is Native American. We want kids to understand that this classroom in itself is a mini culture and that when we look at the universals of cultures they are all played out here in this classroom or mini society.

Angie and Nancy's students also depicted how this was apparent in the classroom. These students appreciated the structure provided.

The teachers in our studies made concerted efforts to model and sustain a culture of caring and belonging in their classrooms. They instilled the norm that all team members would strive to understand others' differences and use positive ways for dealing with their conflicts. Some teams included conflict resolution in the curriculum as a way to create respectful interactions. Students were expected to use conflict resolution skills when dealing with classroom disagreements. This expectation contributed to a safe, secure place for students and their belongings. Further, it reinforced the skills necessary for them to interact respectfully with others and successfully deal with conflict in the world outside the classroom. For some students, this classroom experience was the only positive modeling of conflict resolution they encountered.

A sixth-grader on Sarah and Betsy's team described how learning conflict resolution skills impacted the way students interacted with their teammates.

> If the teachers see us arguing they make us use conflict resolution. That is hard sometimes because you can be so angry, but they will come over and say, "Wait, you know a different way to do this." We might not want to do this, but we all get along a lot better now that we use conflict resolution.

A seventh-grade student on Erica and Shannon's team felt the conflict resolution skills had practical value. "I actually use it outside of the school. My Dad and I just disagree a lot so we use conflict resolution a lot." The power of modeling respectful behavior is well illustrated in an example from Angie and Nancy's classroom. One humid Friday in June ended with some students' losing control. Angie and Nancy called a class meeting to discuss the incident. Angie pointed out that the many special activities that occur at the end of the school year cause chaos if students don't use their group skills, and she reminded the students that she and Nancy were always there to help them. In keeping with the culture of respect they worked to embody in their classroom, these teachers delivered the message in a very respectful tone and manner. Children were not blamed, singled out, or chastised. On the contrary, the teachers acknowledged the pressure on students resulting from a change in the normal classroom routine and were gently yet firmly reminded of the skills to use in solving conflicts. It is apparent through teacher and student voice that basic respect for self and others guided all of their interactions.

Learning

Just as teachers and students identified a sense of belonging as a central outcome for students on these teams, so too did they describe the enhanced learning in their classrooms as a significant benefit of partner teams. Teachers and students in this study perceived five ways through which the partner team positively influenced students' learning: increasing clarity and consistency; possessing control over time; making curricular connections; including students with special needs; and communicating more immediately and effectively with parents.

Clarity and consistency. Yvonne expressed her feelings about the value of the consistency that she and Lori provide for their students. "Students have fewer personalities to deal with; they know what to expect from us. They have less coping to do, and we have them for two years; so there is not the usual transition problem from one grade to the next."

The partnership forged by two teachers resulted in an environment that supported and sustained student learning. Nancy described how her relationship with Angie played out in the classroom. "Students constantly see us model different strategies, different learning styles. They see us solve problems and use conflict resolution skills in a respectful way. They also see that we don't agree on everything but that we work it out." Conversations with students in Nancy and Angie's class confirmed these teachers' efforts to consistently model collaborative, cooperative behavior. Observations also confirmed the consistency with which they operated throughout the day.

Whether they were working together or separately, they both practiced these behaviors:

- Consistently set time limits for activities or tasks, with a warning before the time was up
- Recognized students who were ready to begin the activity

- Provided directions for what students should do if they should finish their individual or group tasks early, with these guidelines always given before the activity started

- Reminded students of what they should be doing, rather than what they were not doing

- Required the attention of the entire group before beginning instructions

- Worked from an agenda or outline on the board for their lesson

- Expected students to leave the room orderly when the class was over.

Control over time. Flexibility in scheduling is a key characteristic of effective middle schools. These partner teams had control over their schedules and the way they organized for instruction. Because students remained in one place for all of their main subjects, time normally spent passing from class to class was captured for instruction. Lori pointed out the advantage of time spent in the classroom rather than in transition. "With seventh and eighth graders, every transition is an opportunity to become excitable. So the fewer transitions, the better off they are. And, with our block schedule they have fewer transitions in their day."

Students, too, were very aware of the impact this extra time had on their learning. One comment from a sixth grader on Sarah and Betsy's team illustrated her understanding of how the time, or the lack of it, influenced her learning.

> It's easier to be on this team because you don't switch around as much; you can ask more questions, and you can get more help like during writing workshop or catch-up time. If you need to know something you have the time to go to the teacher and ask because you don't have to keep looking at the clock. You have as long as you need to take.

Of all the issues students discussed, they felt strongest about the difference the increased time had on the way they were learning. Most striking to the students was that they did not feel rushed as they had in previous years. There was a sense that they had time to really understand a concept and to get extra help if they were having trouble.

This team-based control over time and schedule was not without some drawbacks, however. While students appreciated the quality of the friendships with students on their team, many lamented the lack of contact, except during specials, or unified arts, and lunch with those students not on their team. For the teachers, a long block of time meant that students with challenging behaviors were ever present. They all agreed, however, that the positive outcomes far outweighed the negatives.

One of the most fundamental outcomes resided in the opportunities for curriculum transformation and improved relationships. A sixth-grade student in Sarah and Betsy's class voiced that the increased time teachers and students spent together allowed them to get to know one another on a more intimate level. This familiarity allowed them to feel comfortable and safe enough to express their disagreement with teachers when they felt differently about something.

> If you are only in a class for 45 minutes, you don't
> really know them, and you are not going to have time
> to say "No, I can do this a different way." The thing
> is here you feel more comfortable with the teachers,
> and if someone takes offense or really disagrees with
> something, that person will tell the teacher, and she
> won't get angry, and they can talk about it.

The freedom to take the intellectual risk of disagreeing with the teacher, of challenging conventional wisdom in an effort to find a different way to solve a problem or identify a cause, is an essential part of educating students for a democratic society. As Dewey (1962) argued, schools can and should offer learners freedom in interaction based on the fundamental principles of democracy. The effective partner teams in this study were able to build this safe climate of risk taking and disagreement. The climate in turn provided opportunities for using a variety of curriculum approaches and practicing democratic principles.

Curricular connections. In addition to autonomy over the schedule, having only two people responsible for the four major subjects has a strong impact on approaches to curriculum. Since the two teachers were responsible for all areas, the subjects were typically taught as parts of an overall organizing theme or were paired: science with math, and social studies with language arts, most commonly. The teachers saw and could make natural connections between disciplines, connections between which they may have been previously unaware. Betsy was nothing less than ebullient when she described the curricular connections she and Sarah could achieve on their team.

> It is just so much easier to integrate material when you are with the same students and you know them well. Some days we just amaze ourselves how things fit in together. You can bring and relate what you talked about this morning in the afternoon. And we just sort of sit back and say, "Wow, that was good!"

Rather than learning each subject discretely, the two-teacher team structure allowed students to see how the subjects supported and connected with one another. One of Betsy and Sarah's students described how these connections were made between subjects and with the real world.

> The teachers like to make what they call connections with different subjects. They combine like fractions and economy or whatever the two things we are studying in different subjects like science and math or math and social studies. What was due today was fractions with writing and it was a story about fractions. Also in our newspaper study, they find questions in the newspaper, things that they could ask related to the newspaper in all of our subjects that we have been studying. They combine things with world issues.

Another student also speculated why connections between subjects were difficult to make on larger teams that moved from class to class each period. "One reason I think teachers don't make connections is that they just teach science all day and have to make sure the classes are at about the same place. But here we can combine subjects because they are the teachers all the time."

Students felt that a higher level of learning was achieved on their two-teacher team than on their former teams. One seventh-grader attributed the in-depth study of his subjects to not having to switch classes.

> One thing is that, in other classes, the teachers only have 45 minutes with what they are talking about. With the time it takes to get settled and then get ready to leave at the end the teacher will really have only about 30 minutes. But we can take a whole hour or an hour and a half to discuss something if we are really interested in it.

Beane (1997) has defined curriculum integration as focused on enhancing the opportunities for personal and social integration through the organization of curriculum based on real-life problems and issues without regard for discipline-specific boundaries. Students on partner teams make such connections readily, especially since there are only two teachers standing by to facilitate the associations between life experiences and new learnings.

Inclusion of students with special needs. Another advantage of working with only one other adult was the team's capacity to integrate and monitor students with special needs into all classroom activities. Ed expressed the advantage succinctly. "A good analogy is a floor with two planks; there is just one crack that you can fall in between with us; whereas with a five-person team, there are five planks with four cracks." Ed's partner Rob elaborated further. "There are fewer places to get lost. They are with Ed or me. So it is easier for the special education teacher to plan assignments or accommodations, as there are not five rooms in five periods." In describing her team's capacity to deal with students with special needs, Sarah used her former experience as a member of a larger team, to explain the advantage of a two-teacher team. "In large teams you might not figure a student out until April. Now, by November I feel like we know all the students well. their learning styles, their patterns of behavior—and we've connected with them all."

Betsy commented on how the increased time with students and input of another helped identify students in need of special services who had slipped through the system. "It is so easy for special needs kids from a middle class family to hide. We have discovered kids that have nice clothes, are clean and articulate, but have learning problems never diagnosed."

Their words connect strongly to the principles that guide policy and legislation for students with disabilities. Focused attention to the special needs of children was possible in these classrooms for two reasons. First, the teachers saw the students functioning in a variety of learning situations over extended periods of time. Second, teachers had the benefit of the insights of the partner to strengthen and enrich their opinion of the students' talents and challenges. Teachers developed a realistic, holistic understanding of the child, enabling him or her to address a student's needs and provide meaningful opportunities for inclusion in daily classroom activities.

Parental communication. Early adolescence is a time when 10 to 15-year-olds' communication with parents declines as the maturing individual expresses independence along with open criticism of elders. At this same time, most young adolescents move from the security of a self-contained classroom to a team of four or more teachers, each with varying expectations and styles. Often, parents feel at a loss in regard to communicating with the school and teachers. Once they could simply contact their child's teacher; now the school seems to present a mysterious combination of personalities and procedures. Partner teams, however, eliminate most transition problems and offer many other solutions. Increased communication between families and teachers is another benefit of partner teaming. The partner teams we studied employed the usual communication tools such as phone calls, report cards, newsletters, back-to-school nights, and parent conferences; but the effectiveness of these traditional means increased substantially as a result of smallness. Other avenues of family involvement were noted in our study. The notion of family had real meaning because parents were involved in goal-setting conferences, served as audience for student presentations, were used as resource persons in the instructional program, and their suggestions were solicited. In those cases where the partner team looped, the benefits to parents, of course, increased dramatically.

Summary

For the participants in our research, the climate of caring and respect created affiliation for young adolescents. The team provided security and a sense of place, a home for students within the larger school. Teachers consistently modeled positive collaboration for students and communicated more immediately and fully with parents. As both teachers and students perceived, the two-teacher structure encouraged curriculum integration, and longer blocks of learning time enhanced the effectiveness of learning opportunities. Students gained access to more than one teaching style without having to negotiate four different sets of expectations. How does one achieve these desirable conditions? Chapter 4 (p. 57) describes considerations for both teachers and administrators who work with partner teams. ⑥

HOPE AND KRISTA

Krista arrives at 7:00 A.M., followed by her student teacher, Gretchen. Both chat happily as they walk in, and as Krista takes her coat off, she notes Gretchen's black dress and her own black skirt. She laughs, "Oh, I hope Hope isn't wearing black today! We tend to dress alike." Her silver earrings flash against her skin, providing sparkle to her already animated, morning demeanor. The open, double classroom is brightly decorated, with student work on the walls, and an organized appearance.

Hope arrives shortly thereafter, and Krista repeats her concern aloud. Hope, too, laughs, stating, "No, I wanted it to be spring today, so I chose yellow." Her face quickly becomes serious, however, as she relates to the two teachers how her young son fell down the stairs in his walker, the evening before. Krista stops what she is doing and gives her undivided attention while the episode is related. "He's going to be all right," Hope is quick to reassure them as she relates the tale, still visibly distressed about the incident.

She walks across their classroom to her desk in the front of the room, next to Krista's. They are both seated, looking through paperwork on their desks and referring to lesson plan books. "Will you be able to give up one of your preps to do magazine planning?" Krista asks Hope. "Oh, of course," Hope replies.

Students begin to straggle in, and as they do, the teachers chat with them. The partners readily include their student teacher in the conversation. It is clear that the three have an easy and comfortable rapport. The teachers write the day's agenda on their blackboards, which face each other from opposite sides of the room. Hope reminds Krista that they need to assign new seats today, and the two of them circle their individual sides of the room, placing yellow post-it notes on desks to inform students of the change. Their students are fifth and sixth graders, who spend two years on this team, and they are mixed on both sides of the room. The teachers spend the remainder of the morning prior to the start of school organizing materials, suggesting jobs that students could do to help the class, and chatting about the evening before.

Hope looks up at the clock and speaks to the students in the room. "All right. It's ten of; find yourself a good book or a journal, your choice." The students respond quickly, moving to accommodate that task, and are soon settled and silent. After ten minutes, the morning announcements are read over the intercom by the principal, teachers, and students. The announcements end, and the students and teachers rise to say the Pledge of Allegiance. As they finish, Krista says, "Have a great day!" The students exit the room on the way to exploratories.

Krista and Gretchen seat themselves at a group of three student desks, preparing for planning time. Hope calls, "I'm almost ready!" She pulls together some papers from her desk and quickly joins them. Because of the addition of the student teacher this semester and the mentoring that it involves, planning this year has been a bit different. Whereas Hope and Krista usually plan their units collaboratively, Hope has taken the lead on creating their Explorers Unit, with Krista and Gretchen taking on supporting roles. They begin their meeting with Hope sharing first. She fills them in on the unit, and what today's and the week's activities will entail. Krista seems very attentive to Hope's large workload, and raises the question, "What do you want us to do?" Hope responds that today they will begin their research on individual explorers in the library, and that they could support her in helping students find answers to the central research questions. She also comments that Krista and Gretchen's task of planning the following week will be helpful. Krista seems startled by this comment, as though this is a change from what she understood. "So you were asking us to come up with lessons and homework for the week? We didn't know that..." Krista's voice trails off. "Yes. Not that I want to put any undue stress on you," Hope assures. "No, we just need some time to organize it." Krista replies; "I feel like I threw you a monkey wrench." "We just didn't understand," Hope explains. "My concern is that I don't think there's a week's worth of material here. We thought you just wanted us to research." Hope replies apologetically but firmly, "Well, I'd like to be able to take this over and say, 'Don't worry about it', but I'm going to feel incredibly swamped if I assume more of this."

Krista nods sympathetically, and the conversation moves on to planning lessons and assignments for their "Me" magazine unit. Krista takes the lead for this portion of the meeting, taking the team down the list of articles. As each teacher assumes responsibility for some of them, depending on interests or background, the conversation is interrupted by the principal's appearance. He drops in to tell them about the upcoming parent night, when each team will present its program and perspective to the community, so that the parents of incoming fifth graders will be able to choose the team they consider right for their children.

Krista appears disturbed by this announcement and asks, "So, this is an executive decision?" As the principal exits, he responds curtly, "No, we've had several conversations about this." Krista shakes her head, frustrated, yet the team returns immediately to planning the magazine unit. Krista and Hope phrase their initial ideas as questions, and build on one another's ideas, by adding to and extending the previous idea. Once they have mutually developed the organizational format for the unit, Krista offers to take the lead on the major task at hand, creating the leveled folders which will be a part of the unit. "I'll work these up and then level the folders if you two will do the others." Hope and Gretchen agree, and they move on to brainstorming the physical management of the project. Once again, one teacher throws out an idea as a question, and the other picks it up, modifying it and extending it. They have quickly determined both the structure and assignments for the unit and end with redefining roles and responsibilities for each team member.

"All right, are we all done?" Krista asks. "I'm still not comfortable with the colonization piece, the explorers..." Hope admits, referring to their misunderstanding at the start of the planning meeting. "Normally we plan as more of a partnership; it's the only way we really function well," she explains to Gretchen." Krista adds, "When we don't get to plan a unit together, this is what happens."

Hope appears reassured, and returns to her desk to finish her preparation for math class. Gretchen and Krista continue to meet about their planning of lessons for next week and the Explorers Unit. Hope offers one or two comments from her desk, and they finish with Krista once again summarizing what they will do next.

The teachers are soon back at their desks, working on individual preparations. From time to time, they chat briefly, with Krista describing her Easter brunch, asking about Hope's upcoming professional conference, and commenting on her busy schedule tomorrow afternoon. Hope brings up the administrator's announcement and reinforces Krista's challenge, stating, "I like how you challenged him." They discuss their dissatisfaction with the way in which the format of the parent night sets teams up to sell themselves, like an "auction block," and they appear most distressed with the principal's belief that it had been a collaborative decision, when they clearly feel that it was not.

The students return at snack time, and from there the team moves into math classes. Hope pulls out the tan, foldable wall in between the wide, double classroom, in order to create a sense of quiet between the two. The students are ability grouped for math and spelling, and heterogeneously grouped for all other lessons. For this math class, the special educator takes the highest ability group into an adjoining room, and Hope and Krista work with the remaining two groups on fractions in individual settings. The students work in these small groups within their ability groups, practicing adding, subtracting, and multiplying fractions in preparation for a quiz tomorrow.

As math class ends, Krista pulls the room divider back. The next activity is Book Club, and the students return to their original seats. Both teachers stand in front of the room, and Hope addresses the class, telling them the order of the upcoming skits, and directing them about where the stage and audience will be. Krista gets the students seated as Hope gets the scripts from the student actors. Perched on desks, the teachers sit side by side behind the audience. Hope assesses the skits as they are performed, which are appreciated with applause and laughter from the class.

The classroom telephone rings, and Hope answers, speaks briefly and hangs up. She passes the evaluation forms to Krista quickly and wordlessly, and exits the room. Krista picks up where Hope left off, jotting assessment notes down as the skits progress. When the performances finish, Krista announces, "Okay, those of you who performed today should use this time to self-assess, and those of you who did not should use this time to practice your skits. I'm not sure exactly what she had planned next, so she may come back and change it, but I think this is it."

Hope returns shortly, and says, "Thanks, Krista. I'm assuming the kids on this side are assessing?" Krista nods and fills her in on the progress of the class. They walk around the room together, assisting students and discussing Hope's phone conversation with the superintendent of schools regarding the parent-conference schedule. The students continue to work, and Krista exits to use the restroom. Hope looks around to see both the student teacher and a classroom assistant working with students in the room. Assured that there is adequate supervision, she too exits, and finds Krista in the restroom.

"I'm so sorry about the misunderstanding we had earlier with the Explorers Unit. It's hard to function when we are not planning together. I miss that time. When you and Gretchen were planning together after our meeting, I felt like that should've been me!" Hope laughs as she says this, but is clear and up front about her feelings. Krista agrees, and they share a hug before returning to the classroom together, refocused on the task at hand.

The next activity is a read-aloud before lunchtime. While Krista perches on a stool in front of her desk and reads aloud from *Watership Down*, students gather around her on the floor and on comfortable couches. They are attentive and interested, although a few whisper and giggle in one corner from time to time. Students move from that activity to lunch, and the teachers gather around a group of student desks to eat lunch and chat.

The conversation is comfortable from the start; the teachers discuss their families and how they are managing to juggle their personal and professional lives. Hope is the mother of two boys, both of whom are toddlers. Krista's son is a freshman in high school, and she remembers clearly the challenges that Hope is facing with a young family.

Krista shares her evening plans with Hope and Gretchen as she talks about one boy in their class whose family has been recently evicted from the trailer park. Now living temporarily with his family in a motel, he has contracted strep throat. Krista is concerned about him, and upon asking his mother about medical care for him, has been told the family could not afford it. Krista asked the mother if she would sign a waiver to allow her to take him to a physician, and the mother did so.

As lunch comes to a close, the students return for indoor recess. Hope directs them to certain activities, and they busy themselves with these, undisturbed by the unseasonable weather. One of the chalkboards shows the students' brainstormed list of signs of spring. On the list are ideas about spring attributes: longer days, melting snow, plants coming up, my mother's happier, frisky pets, skunks, and lambs. It is hard to imagine any of these harbingers of spring as the fat white flakes of snow fall wetly onto the ground outside the window. Inside, however, spring has arrived full-force as the students chirp like lively birds, and the walls are decorated with bright colors.

Hope gathers the class together once more and begins the Explorers Unit by asking the students what comes to mind when they think about the term *exploration*. Students are eager to respond, raising their hands and suggesting names such as Neil Armstrong and Christopher Columbus. While Hope conducts this introductory activity, Krista sits in the back of the room at a computer, grateful for the time to compose a letter to the superintendent on behalf of both of them. At the same time, she monitors student behavior at the back of the room. As the students move on to make a list of why they would choose to colonize the moon, who they would send, and what they would do upon arrival, Hope and Krista effortlessly switch places. Hope moves to the back of the room to proofread the letter on the computer, while Krista rotates to the front of the room. As the students complete the activity, they share their answers with the class, categorizing as they go. Hope writes their answers on the chart pad, while Krista helps to categorize. This integrated study period continues throughout the afternoon, until the school day comes to a close. Krista and Hope circulate as the students find their seats and wait for dismissal.

As the bells ring for busses and walkers, students rise with backpacks stuffed with books and papers and place their chairs on top of their desks. As the last bus is called, the teachers sit at their desks, compiling files and papers. They say their good-byes, and Krista rushes off to the faculty talent show rehearsal before her after-school plans with their student, while Hope leaves to pick up her sons on her way home. •

4

FORMING A NEW TEAM: WHAT SHOULD BE CONSIDERED?

*True belonging is born of relationships not only to one
another but to a place of shared responsibilities and
benefits. We love not so much what we have acquired
as what we have made and whom we have made it
with. —* Robert Finch, *The Primal Place*

Each year, in middle schools across the nation, new teams are
formed. Faculty members retire or move to new positions, a
bubble in the student population calls for additional slots, or
existing teams need to be reconstituted. In any case, administrators
regularly find themselves responsible for forming new teams. How
is team membership determined? What typically weighs in on the
decision? What factors should one really consider?

Historically, team members have been identified by discipline,
often the sole criterion for membership. In the departmentalized
junior high model, or even traditional middle schools, teams have
been comprised of one teacher per "core" academic area, sometimes
with a reading teacher added as a fifth teacher. Experience and
common sense tell us there is more to consider than the prime
academic disciplines, particularly when the middle school concept
is being implemented. The effective team members in our study
suggest there are at least five elements critical in creating new teams:
*teacher choice, a shared belief system, a personal connection,
complementary strengths,* and *a common work ethic.*

Choosing a partner

As is evidenced in the four vignettes interspersed throughout this text, partner team members work very closely together, day in and day out. It is therefore essential that the teachers have a voice in the pairing process. Hope expressed the importance of teacher choice in this way. "If you are really going into teaming, you want to choose a partner carefully. It's not something you take lightly, because it can either make or break your career as a professional educator." When we asked the other teachers what advice they would give a person who was considering partner teaming, the need for having a voice in the selection and hiring process was on everybody's list.

> You have got to find the right teammate…I hear over
> and over again, "I would love to do what you are
> doing, but I can't because there isn't anybody wanting
> or willing to take the risk of changing his or her style
> of teaching." You need to find somebody that you can
> work with.

For Hope, Krista's belief in the importance of this choice resulted in her obtaining the position. "Krista asked me to be her teammate. She felt there was good rapport between the two of us, and we had the beginnings for a good team; so she advocated for me, and I got my job." Ted's advice was short and succinct: "Find the right person." Brief though it was, this advice is fundamental.

While self-selection is important, team composition is more often than not determined by the principal who is faced with many valid considerations, including certification. At times, he or she will reassign teachers from a highly functional team to ones that are floundering in hopes new team members will transform the struggling teams. Principals, however, can and should approach team membership selection in a positive and affirming manner. An important application of effective leadership is empowering partner teams to self-select. There are clear and impressive benefits to team self-selection. Teams who selected their own members or who exercised significant influence over team membership have been found to spend significant time engaged in team planning and coordination (Mac Iver, 1990). In the fields of business and industry, as well, a team's probability of success increases if it is well chosen from the beginning and receives appropriate training. Allowing the team to have input into member selection results in a greater commitment by the entire team to curriculum integration and success of a new member (Darrell & Bronstein, 1995).

Research from the field of business also provides helpful information on the personality traits that potential team members should consider during the team selection process. Driskell (1988), for example, developed a structure to predict the interaction between personality variables and team tasks. His research identified six personality traits affecting team performance: (1) intelligence, (2) adjustment, (3) ambition, (4) prudence, (5) sociability, and (6) likability. Driskell also developed a framework for predicting the interactive effects of the personality traits on the different tasks. For example, a team member who ranked high on adjustment, sociability, and likability would be selected for tasks requiring supportive social skills. Further, in a study of airline crews, Foushee (1984) found that personal compatibility strongly influenced team effectiveness for groups who worked long hours in confined quarters (conditions that certainly could be ascribed to partner teams). Thus, research as well as common sense make it imperative that when selecting team members, the relationship between personalities and the team's required tasks must be a prime consideration. Empowering teachers with input into team membership is the first step toward success for any size team.

Sharing a belief system

Another reason why teachers require a strong voice in partner selection is the importance of having a shared belief system. Having a common philosophy was a major ingredient in the glue that held the teachers' relationship together. It guided most of the interactions they had with each other and with their students. It informed their decision making and, ultimately, made it possible for the partnership to function in an effective manner.

Although there have been few studies exclusively on partner teams, the co-teaching literature from the field of special education offers both research and helpful theoretical frameworks in understanding the nature of collaborative work. A shared philosophy appears in co-teaching as being central to the success of collaborative endeavors (ERIC Digest, 1993; Friend & Cook, 1992; Harris, 1990).

Similarly, the teachers in our study spoke of the need to share a vision of what education should be like for students and of what happens when this vision is not shared. As they described their current teaming relationships, teachers returned to this concept again and again. Hope stressed, "When the two of us get into the classroom, we are really in sync when it comes to what we believe in and how we are going to get there and why we want to get there." When asked to define an effective team member, Krista drew upon this need immediately. "Somebody who thinks the same way about kids. We could not do what we do if we didn't believe the same things about kids and what kids are capable of." As they reflected on prior teaming experiences, teachers also spoke of the sometimes devastating impact of not sharing a vision. As Shannon put it, "We've been on four-person teams with people who had a different vision of education and kids. It is very difficult to work under those circumstances, and the students suffer." Shannon echoed the research literature on interdisciplinary teaming that asserts where teachers share a common vision they have a feeling of efficacy (Lee, Dedrick, & Smith, 1991).

Sarah highlighted the influence a shared philosophy has on the decision-making process and how it relates to teachers' limited time during the school day.

> One obvious thing about including more than one person in a decision is the greater amount of time it takes. And when you don't have much time, then you really need a shared philosophical base. We understand each other's approach enough so that we don't spend a lot of time backing up to square one on every decision. Our shared philosophy allows us to effectively use our limited time making decisions.

These teachers' common philosophical groundings are striking yet become even more so when one considers specific elements of the commonalities. As the teachers spoke, it became clear that there were two tenets particularly consistent across all teams: first, students came first in their priorities—what Erica called "a kids-first attitude"; and second, these teachers took a holistic approach to the education of these students. When probed further about what these belief systems entailed or included, these effective partner teachers spoke up about the need to place students at the top of their lists.

Heather made clear that this prioritizing impacted the teachers' lives in a variety of ways, not the least of which was by asking their families to make certain sacrifices. Alan emphasized that … "both of our families have sacrificed so we could do what we felt was right for the kids." Erica explained, that because of their priorities, they adjusted the curriculum and the content to fit the needs of students.

These partner teachers spoke of their belief in attending to the needs of the whole child. Shannon expressed it this way:

> We are dealing with the whole child and have a
> very holistic view. We are looking at what goes on
> in a child's whole life and trying to work with those
> circumstances to help him or her achieve success
> rather than just being concerned with the content
> under consideration.

The socio-emotional needs of students have to be addressed if academic learning is to occur. These partner teachers shared a foundation for decision making as a team. Shared beliefs worked in concert with a personal connection between the teachers.

Connecting personally

Teacher communities, whether they are teams, departments, or whole faculties, differ considerably in how they collaborate and make decisions. A central challenge is to create professional learning communities built upon caring, interdependence, and trust. It is not surprising, then, that in addition to sharing a philosophical grounding, these teachers expressed a genuine fondness for their partners. Krista stated it plainly: "You have to find someone that you can work with, that you can hit it off with and enjoy being with. If you don't genuinely like one another, teaming is not going to work."

Though it may seem obvious, the personal connection between the partners was almost a necessity, given the amount of time spent together. As Ted put it, "I spend more time with John than I do with my wife most school weeks!" Erica made a distinction between a professional relationship and what she referred to as a personal connection.

> It is really critical that you have a personal connection
> with the person. I don't call it a relationship as much

as a connection. I can have a professional relationship
with a number of people. I've been on four-person
teams, and I've had professional relationships with the
people I taught with. That feels much different to me
than the relationship I have in this partnering situation.
Here there is a meshing of philosophies, a trust, a
respect, a confidence.

Both Heather and Ted underscored the need to be friends, yet
were careful to differentiate between this friendship and what one
might consider to be a social relationship. Heather explains,

I don't think you can have a team and not be a friend
of your colleague. You don't have to socialize and
have your entire life wrapped around that person, but
you should have someone whom you are involved
with outside, someone whom you talk about your own
kids or family, and sometimes socialize with.

Ted's comments echoed Heather's perspective,

If I were interviewing a prospective team member, I
would look for somebody whom I felt like I could be
friends with. Like John and I don't spend all our free
time together. We rarely meet on weekends. Once in a
while we'll see each other socially, but it's infrequent.
But it would have to be somebody whom I would
enjoy spending time with.

Erica inserted her thoughts on the need for this connection
in relation to their content backgrounds. "You look at personal
connection first, then the curriculum. It is easier to forge curriculum
than a relationship. The relationship lays the groundwork for forging
curriculum and using the strengths and backgrounds of each partner."

Possessing complementary strengths

The co-teaching literature from the field of special education
again provides us with a helpful context for thinking about the work
of partner teachers. Adams and Cessna (1993) offer their third and
final metaphor, yin and yang, to depict both the uniqueness of and
the unity between two teachers. Each teacher brings to the classroom

his or her individual strengths and skills, and these attributes join together in harmony to create a whole, the sum of the individual parts. This metaphor aptly describes the partner team. As they explored their own partnerships, these teachers identified their complementary strengths as a key to their effectiveness.

Research on strong marriages offers insight and understanding into the importance of teammates' possessing complementary strengths. Couples in strong marriages achieve a balance between the need to be intimate and the need to maintain individuality. They are aware of the differences in their personalities and how those differences manifest themselves and strengthen their partnership. Certainly, the teams in our studies achieved that healthy balance between team and self. They understand the unique skills and approaches each one brought and how they could work in concert.

The relationships that individuals develop in the workplace are influenced by the same aspects of personal development that influence interactions within a family. Just as the family is affected by the behavior of each individual, the workplace is also affected. Though the quality of the workplace is certainly influenced by the maturity of the leader, it is equally influenced by each individual's level of differentiation. Workers with higher levels of differentiation help create a work system that is efficient and productive. The mature individual has developed a balance between maintaining a distinct sense of self and the need to be an accepted and approved member of a group. It is this balance that is central to the relational work of partner teams.

Within these partnerships, the two teachers tended to take different approaches in a variety of circumstances. When dealing with students or parents, when solving problems or analyzing situations, or when planning curriculum, their difference in approach actually assisted them in moving forward. Hope spoke of the balance she appreciated between the two of them. "I tend to be more logical, while Krista really runs with an idea. She is quick; when she is on a roll she is incredible. I tend to be the one that needs to chunk it out. So I see that as being a good balance, as I can hold the reins sometimes."

Alan described the way he and Heather operate: "When it comes to the actual planning, we do that together; but she does the paperwork for us because she is more organized than I am. I'm more visual; once I see it in my head I know what I want to do, while she needs to have it in black and white."

Understanding these differences is an important consideration in forming teams. To enhance team members' awareness of the diverse approaches they can use, there are a number of commercially prepared inventories that can help partner teams both understand and appreciate the reasons why their partners approach tasks and situations the way they do. Gathering data about individual cognitive styles and learning approaches is also important. The more information team members have on one another, the greater the opportunity for resolving potential conflicts and enhancing collaboration. *The Myers-Briggs Type Indicator* (Kirby & Myers, 2000), for example, is a self-reporting questionnaire that identifies differences between people, which can be the source of misunderstanding and miscommunication if not identified and understood. *The Cognitive Styles Inventory* (Gregoric, 1982; Butler, 1986), also a self-reporting inventory, is based on two dimensions: 1) *remote association,* which is a skill in making rapid, non-logical, and intuitive connections between given elements, thus accelerating the process of problem solving; and 2) *differentiation,* which is the ability of people with a discriminating eye to identify and fixate on discrepancies in theory or empirical evidence. Such people can work with messy subjective criteria and an ill-structured task environment. Depending on their cognitive style, people have different orientations and preferences. These instruments, or others available, can assist teachers in gaining important insights about themselves that will allow them to understand, support, and celebrate the different strengths each brings to a partner team.

Less idiosyncratic than differing approaches and styles, but no less important, are the different content backgrounds that partners bring to the team. The teachers in our study were quick to point out that their strengths in different disciplines enabled them to provide a more comprehensive picture for students. Hope, for instance, noted: "Professionally, we complement each other. Krista has more of a language arts background, and I have more of a math and science background. When you put the two of us together you get a pretty tight package able to handle the content." Complementary content area backgrounds obviously assist the teams in planning curricula.

Heather illustrated this in her example of a recently planned thematic unit.

> Sometimes Alan sees connections that I don't see.
> Like one of the kids for the Future Unit wanted to
> deal with winning the Megabucks. And I thought,
> "What?" But Alan was able to say, "Well, we can look
> at probability, statistics." And he helped the kid plan a
> whole Megabucks activity that involved a drawing and
> serious discussion about odds. He was able to take the
> kids' idea and fit it into math, whereas I wasn't able to.

Although we describe in greater detail elsewhere the importance and results of making these essential connections within and across curricula, we note it here to underscore that complementary content areas is one of many important factors to consider when forming new teams. The teachers went beyond recognizing and celebrating their differences; they acknowledged how differences actually enriched their relationship. One teacher's strength compensated for the other's weakness. In the daily running of the team, the differences in personalities covered both the details and the broad picture. The teachers were also aware that their understanding of each other's differences changed and deepened over time. Their recognition and appreciation of professional differences extended to basic personality traits, acknowledging that personal attributes influence professional ones. These teachers knew that they could not be artificially separated if they were to work and learn together.

Holding a common work ethic

Work ethic as a construct is often highlighted in business. Within education, as well, attention to work ethic has emerged as important in the attainment of an educational mission (Kleinsmith & Everts-Rogers, 2000). The partner teachers in our studies resoundingly described the need for a common work ethic. Ted asserted,

> Having a sense of equity as far as the workload goes
> is important so you don't feel like the person is doing
> less or more than his or her share. I remember a couple
> of people who intimidated me because they were so
> hardworking and such perfectionists. And there have
> been other people I felt weren't carrying their share.

They had different expectations about what a teacher should be doing.

The need for a common work ethic certainly played a role in team member selection. Krista said she always raised a question in interviews: How much time outside the classroom could you give? Some people were very restrictive about what they were willing to share and give up and that needed to be identified up front. Nancy's description of the amount of time she and Angie spent in thinking, talking, and planning highlighted the importance of a common work ethic in such a close relationship.

> Even when I'm home with my husband and two children, I'm thinking about things here in the classroom. Sunday nights we call each other and talk for an hour and run through everything for the entire week. We want to make sure we know what we're doing, and that takes time.

The work demands placed on two teachers responsible for the entire curriculum and for 40-60 students for most of the day required both teachers to work very hard. Implicit in the teachers' reflections was an extraordinary sense of responsibility to each other and to their students.

Summary

The perspectives and reflections of these teachers speak clearly to anyone involved in creating new teams. First and foremost, team members must have a voice in choosing their partners. Then, the following questions must be considered: Do the teachers hold compatible beliefs about education and kids? Do they bring differing, yet complementary strengths to the team? Will the teachers put in equal amounts of time and energy? Answering positively to these questions places a new team on a solid road for effectiveness. It is not, however, the sure-fire prescription to long-term success. Once established, there is an intense and ongoing need to maintain and sustain the relationship. This maintenance comes internally from the partner teachers themselves and through external support from the school administration or others. We describe these factors in Chapter 5 (p. 72), sharing teachers' perspectives on how to nurture and support a team. ⑥

ERICA AND SHANNON

The early April morning feels more like February as Erica steps into her car, noticing her breath in the air. She drives over to Shannon's house, a convenient "two dirt roads behind her." Shannon is ready, and they begin their teaming day together, as usual, by carpooling. They lament the lack of time that the school day provides for critical reflection and find their early morning talks on the way to school one more way to fit in the needed conversations.

As she rides in the passenger seat, Shannon expresses her concern with the way their reporting-out system is not as reflective of individual growth as she would like. "If you really believe in taking kids from where they are and moving them along at their own pace and individual progress, which we do, then grading them during the first semester makes no sense. We should just be providing narrative reports."

"In fact, we shouldn't be grading them during either semester, for that matter." Erica is quick to add. As the car whizzes by tapped sugar maples that are unresponsive to the weather, they continue to express frustration in the conflict they feel between what they believe is ethical and what school policies dictate. Their conversation moves on to reviewing for the day what they have planned previously, and they arrive at school already deep in thought and functioning closely as partners.

They park the car and enter the building, greeting students and teachers alike. Then they are off to their respective teacher advisory groups, a practice which both their middle and high schools have long embraced. Each advisory contains approximately ten students and lasts for 20 minutes. Erica meets with her group in a room just off the cafeteria, with large windows and round tables. Shannon holds her group in their partnering space—called "the community building" because the community built it over the summer due to the space crunch at the school. The advisory period has a casual feel, but a serious mission. The teachers touch base with their advisees, making sure things are going well academically, emotionally, and socially. The students also chat among themselves. The time is short, and the students scurry off to their first classes, while Shannon walks over to Erica's space for a team meeting.

This team meeting is a time for the two teachers to inform Suzanne, the special educator assigned to their team, of the plans for the day. Because

Suzanne is an integral part of the teaching day, they take time to talk through their schedule and homework, as well as review the progress of several students. Today, Robert, a seventh grader from Erica's advisory, has joined them in order to complete his map of Australia. From time to time during the meeting, they joke with Robert in a good-natured way, his grin appearing readily each time.

Erica passes a pile of papers to both Suzanne and Shannon, asking, "Why am I missing two Australia quizzes?" They often divide their 34 students into three heterogeneous "family groups" for instructional and record-keeping purposes; each of the teachers will return the quizzes to students in her family group. They discuss among themselves who had missed the quiz and determine a make-up time for those students. They also use the time to collaboratively assess a student's assignment and focus in general on missing assignments before moving on to discuss the plans for the day.

Today they introduce two new projects: their "Who Cares?" project, which asks students to take action on something of importance to them; and their children's book project, which will have every student write, illustrate, and construct a children's book for a younger student in the community. Because the book project will be worked on to some degree in family groups, Erica and Shannon describe the construction process to Suzanne, adding to and expanding on one another's ideas and explanations. When one falters with a word or thought, the other steps in easily to supply it. Each also looks to the other for confirmation from time to time, asking, "Right?" with the other nodding and affirming. There is a clear delineation of roles in the process, with Shannon taking responsibility for construction and binding, and Erica overseeing the writing process. Their planning period comes to an end, and the three teachers make their way back through the winding hallways to their separate "community building" spaces.

Built only nine months earlier, the building is set up like two adjoining classrooms, with rolling bulletin boards dividing them. The space is student designed. Previously, a local woodworker had come in to the class to work with the students. He asked the students to describe what the space would look like if they could have anything they'd like. The students spoke of a loft, a swing, and window seats, all of which he then led them to build in this spacious, light-filled spot.

As Erica, Shannon, and Suzanne enter, the students who have already arrived call out, "Are we having family group today?" and their teachers respond, "Yup!" The students quickly gather in the family groups; and

Shannon, Erica, and Suzanne go to their students and return homework to them. Shannon writes the day's schedule on the chalkboard. The groups function effectively side-by-side; they are accustomed to the family group configuration and are not distracted by the group next to them. Erica reads to her group a pair of postcards sent by a student's parents, and, when finished, says, "Okay. I'm going to write what we're going to do today on the board. She turns around to see that Shannon has already accomplished this task for them. She smiles and gives a quick laugh, asking, "Shannon, are you about set for the map check-up test?" Shannon nods almost imperceptibly as she shuffles though papers in her hand.

"We're going to do our map check-up today in family groups, okay?" Shannon calls out to her group. Erica hears this and echoes it to the students in front of her. Students cram in some last minute studying, then begin the test. Erica meets with one girl about the work she will need to do while she is absent. Shannon, meanwhile, monitors the whole room. "If you know anything else, besides what's on the list, put it down for possible credit," Shannon encourages. She moves soundlessly to switch places with Erica, and adds to the soon-to-be-absent student's work list. As students finish their tests, they turn them over and take out a book to read. The bright sun from the windows shines in, throwing beams of light boldly on the walls, dust dancing in its rays. Erica circulates through the whole room, collecting tests and reminding the students to stay quiet while others finish. Suzanne's family group from the other side of the open building now joins the other two, with all of the students crowding into one area. Erica praises the smooth transition.

Shannon and Erica stand together in front of the room. "I'd like to...," Shannon stops and corrects her use of pronoun, "We'd like to talk to you about a project, which will help you feel like empowered people." The two of them then describe the "Who Cares?" project to the class, giving examples of past projects, including an eighth-grade lunchroom sit-in to gain a longer lunch period, and letters to the U.S. Congress protesting various actions. Shannon has brought in three articles for the students to read in order to expose them to a variety of issues about which they might choose to take action. Shannon takes the lead in asking students to read aloud to the class from an article on Navajo and Hopi land disputes; Erica circulates among them. The teachers relate a story of getting lost as they drove cross-country together with their families. As they discuss the articles as a group, the teachers' partnering abilities are clear. They ask questions and field answers together, encouraging discussion, taking turns effortlessly.

As the time slips quickly away, Shannon says, "Reassemble here after break," and the students disperse. Several students gather around the teachers, asking about assignments or just chatting.

Erica calls out, "Does anyone want a pear? It's good for you!" Seeing no takers at the moment, she sets it down on her desk. She, Shannon, and Suzanne head to the cafeteria for coffee. Shannon is detained on the way, as she stops a student to talk about the student's mother, and catches up with the others moments later. As they sit in the bright cafeteria watching students socialize, their conversation centers around special education and placement options for the upcoming school year.

They return to their building after break, with many students alongside. Erica offers her pear once more, and suddenly four girls all decide they would like it. Erica encourages them to share it, and moves quickly to address the class. As she begins to describe the process of constructing the children's books, she falters in her explanation, her voice trailing off. Shannon picks up immediately and continues the description of the process, with Erica nodding and affirming her words. They divide the students into smaller groups, depending upon the tasks to be accomplished, and one group goes to the other side of the partition.

Erica suddenly remembers a co-worker who also works with these students, who is house-bound with a pulled hamstring. She suggests they call her to let her know they miss her. "We better call Paula. Let's call Paula!" Shannon picks up on this cue, and dials her number, while Erica works with students.

Shannon chats for a minute or so on the phone. After asking Paula about her health, Shannon reminds her, "If you need any help, give us a call; seriously, if you need a ride or anything. Feel better. I'm going to put Erica on."

Shannon returns to help students, while Erica talks with her. Abruptly, she turns to the class, and says, "Kids, let's say 'Hi!' to Paula! One, two, three..." The students ring out, "Hi Paula!" in an exuberant chorus of voices, and then continue with their work at hand for the remainder of the core time. As lunch time arrives, the students clean up their materials, gather their backpacks in anticipation of the specials that await them in the afternoon, and exit the community building. Erica and Shannon, too, leave the building and make their way to the cafeteria.

Their "true" partner teaming, as they put it, ends at lunchtime, as both Shannon and Erica are assigned to teach high school courses in the afternoon within the science and English departments. Shannon and Erica chat as they go through the lunch line in the cafeteria and then find an empty table where Suzanne joins them minutes later. They choose to eat in the cafeteria, rather than the faculty room, because it gives them a little more time for planning and reflection, to keep an eye on many of their students, and to avoid an "incessant talker" who eats in the faculty room. The trio discusses the learning styles of the students, commenting that two of their students in particular simply do not seem to learn the way they are being taught; and they surmise about ways to reach these students.

As lunchtime ends, Shannon returns to the community building to teach a general science class to freshman students, and Erica runs off to attend a department meeting. They are disappointed with the administration's lack of interest in implementing teaming at the high school level. When possible, each teacher tries to remain in the classroom anyway, assisting the other with her class in a variety of ways, unless department meetings dictate that she be elsewhere.

As the school day draws to an end, and they have taught their high school classes, Shannon and Erica are together once more, driving to a nearby store to get coffee. They return to the community building, where they are surrounded by many of the middle level faces they saw earlier in the day. The teachers stay after school to assist students with any schoolwork, lending a hand where necessary. The atmosphere is welcoming, yet businesslike. As the last student leaves, the two pile back into Erica's car to begin the journey home, reflecting on the day's progress, and revising their plans for the next. •

5

KEEPING THE TEAM ON TRACK: WHAT IS REQUIRED?

Beware of enterprises that require new clothes and not rather a new wearer of clothes. — Henry David Thoreau

Assume that the newly selected team members have a shared belief system and a common work ethic. They like each other; they chose one another; and, of course, they have varied areas of expertise and competence. The essential conditions are in place. Now what?

Common planning time, shared students, block schedules, and team space do not make effective teams. These elements are to effective teaming as memorizing lines is to a successful play production. They are essential, but hardly sufficient. Indeed, the interpretation of a part in a play begins after the lines are memorized. So it is with effective teaming: the real work of conversing, negotiating, and decision making begins to take place after the aforementioned foundational elements are in place. (Dickinson & Erb, 1997, p.61)

Although an administrator may have been attentive to complementary strengths, to teacher choice, to a common work ethic, and to mutual philosophies, it is not enough for a team to be thoughtfully and intentionally constructed and left alone. In order to function smoothly, the team must enjoy both internal and external support and be committed to maintaining the health of the teaming relationship. The school's administrative leadership must be equally committed to supporting the team and its initiatives. What is required, then, for a team just formed to function effectively?

Team member attributes

Members of effective teams bring personal attributes to the group that assist them in functioning collaboratively. Teachers on the teams we studied were quick to point out the importance of humor, flexibility, trust, and respect. According to Krista, humor plays a big role in sustaining a healthy relationship. "A good sense of humor is critical. You have to be able to laugh at yourselves and laugh at what the kids are saying and doing—even as our best plans are falling apart." For these teachers, humor helped maintain a positive approach. Ted expressed the need for humor not only in sustaining his love of teaching, but also in modeling for students.

> I think humor is a real key. They see us enjoying teaching. We are having a good time, joking occasionally and kidding each other. It makes for a situation where the kids feel like this is a nice place to be, where the teachers like each other and like teaching. If the teachers are happy, then your school is going to be in pretty good shape.

The teachers also identified flexibility as an important element that maintains the health of their relationship. Alan surmised, "The biggest thing that makes me effective as a team member is flexibility. Not having to follow a strict time line. If Heather needs a few more minutes, that doesn't upset me." For them, flexibility meant a general sense of give and take, being able to perform the roles of the other partner, being willing to see things in an alternate way, and not being overly protective of one's instructional time." Ted added, "We do a lot of planning as the kids are working and adjust time accordingly."

In a study of co-teaching between regular and special educators in a single classroom (Sage, 1995), teachers recognized the importance of a trusting open relationship as critical to developing a culture where they were willing to explore their differences and discuss them openly. The teachers in our study reached similar conclusions. They saw the elements of respect and trust as inherently intertwined. With a foundation of respect, they came to trust the other's judgment on instructional approaches, to make decisions more easily, to trust the other implicitly when dealing with conflicts, and to feel safe in asking the other for support. According to Alan, "Heather doesn't pressure me into doing something that I'm not comfortable with, and I wouldn't pressure her. We have a general respect for each other's feelings and know what the comfort level is."

Hope and Krista found their respect for one another enabled them to mediate two slightly different teaching approaches. Hope described, "Krista tends to be more toward student-centered education. I tend to be more teacher-centered believing that there are some things the kids have to know. But we come to a middle ground. We both respect our different opinions; and when combined, we achieve a really good product."

Ted also reflected on this ability to trust the other's judgment as facilitating their decision making. "One of the reasons we are able to make decisions quickly is because we trust each other. If John suggests something, I readily agree, and vice versa. That way we don't have to debate everything to death and look at all the possible pros and cons."

The high level of trust and respect between the partners provided a sense of predictability about their actions with each other, the students, or other adults. Their energy was not misspent worrying about how their partner would react in a particular situation or with another individual but instead could be used in a more positive application that directly affected their work with students. A trusting, respectful relationship provided the anchor teachers needed to meet the seemingly unrelenting challenges that emerge in the daily life of the middle level classroom.

Communication

The trust and respect that developed on partner teams facilitated and supported a highly developed level of communication. Since the partner teams in our study used the family as a metaphor to describe their relationship with each other and with their students, and each team has been identified as one functioning effectively, it is not surprising that the communication areas described in Olson's (1993) research on healthy families parallel the communication skills present on partner teams. Olson identified five areas necessary for effective communication within a family:

1. Listening skills focus on empathy and attentive listening.

2. Speaking skills involve speaking for oneself and not for others.

3. Self-disclosure relates to sharing feelings about self and relationship.

4. Tracking is staying on topic.

5. Respect and regard relate to being consistently respectful of others' feelings and messages (p.108).

Referred to in the family and marital literature as "communication culture," this concept serves as a metaphor to describe communication in close relationships. It implies that, within relationships, people establish their own means and norms of communicating, including codes and often unspoken sets of rules for interacting (Sillars, 1995). Shannon illustrates the communication culture of her partnership as she describes how they have had to become aware of and adjust to the other's style of communication as their relationship evolved.

> We solve problems by talking them out. I'm the kind of person who processes through discussion, and Erica is the kind of person who processes in her head first. So if something comes up and I immediately want to discuss it, and it is apparent that Erica is not ready to do that, I just end up waiting a little while before we pursue the issue. At the same time, when things come up that I need to talk about now, Erica has gotten to the point where she can just say, "Okay let's talk about it now."

Erica extends this by noting their ability to be clear and up front with their feelings.

> We've both gotten really good about making feeling statements such as, "You know when that happened this morning, that really didn't work for me." Or, "You didn't tell me anything about this, and you took off on this tangent, and I really felt left out of the process."

Not surprisingly, open communication emerged readily as a key behavior critical to a team's success. From Hope's perspective, "Communication has to be the key. To be able to look the person in the eye and tell her what you are thinking without mincing words. Not being able to say what is really on your mind just tears apart any relationship."

Teachers did not take the importance of open, clear, and honest communication for granted. Each partner team member realized that a healthy work environment and an effective relationship were dependent upon his or her willingness to devote the time and attention to ensuring that the air was always clear, and that assumptions were checked and clarified. Time spent by these teams attending to their mutual and individual communication needs paid tremendous dividends in the quality and satisfaction they experienced in their work with each other and with students.

The teams' planning meetings were rich with detail about the teachers' attention to the quality of their communication. The teachers demonstrated a number of behavioral tendencies as they negotiated the work at hand. These tendencies included thinking aloud, phrasing ideas as questions, building on the other's ideas, summarizing responsibilities, being candid about feelings, and stating boundaries. In addition, observing them teaching side by side illustrated the ways they reinforce one another, assist by providing words or ideas, and extend the other's direction or explanation when working with students. The following snapshots are brief representations of these behaviors.

Often, in planning meetings, as the partner teachers began to plan the next unit, they did not come with predetermined plans about how teaching and learning should proceed. Instead, they began the idea development by thinking aloud, often changing their own minds in mid-sentence, altering their own ideas.

Hope and Krista met to discuss their next unit in which students would create magazines about themselves. They came together to determine which articles would be expected of all students, and which would be electives. They weighed the pros and cons of each aspect aloud before coming to conclusions about what would be expected of all and what would be options. Each contributed to the discussion. This practice was not only limited to planning meetings; it appeared in direct teaching moments as well.

Ted and John shared with students the matter of deciding on a topic for their final orbital study of the year. As they did so, they thought through the pros and cons of due dates aloud, quickly reaching consensus. Similarly, John and Ted gathered together briefly, while the students worked independently on spelling words to plan their approach to the novel, *Hatchet*. They reviewed what they had used last year, thinking through their ideas aloud until consensus developed on the plan. These teachers brought ideas to their meetings, not predetermined plans, believing that together they would create a stronger product.

When the teachers arrived at ideas, they often phrased them as questions rather than using declarative or imperative sentences. As Hope and Krista progressed in their magazine unit planning, for example, they began to arrive at tentative decisions and to become more specific with their plans. Hope queried, "Should we present all five assignments on the first day?" This interrogative stance placed her in the position of presenting an idea, while at the same time asking for feedback in a safe and respectful manner.

As the discussion of helping students brainstorm their topics began to wind down, John turned to Ted, quietly asking, "Break here?" This small but natural gesture suggested that decisions were not made autonomously within this team; rather, it was a truly collaborative partnership in which they were both consulted and respected.

As Heather and Alan worked on planning the schedule for the upcoming week, Heather realized they had not provided students with time to work on their drug abuse awareness skits due next week. She suggested in the form of a question, "Do we want to give them D.A.R.E. practice?" rather than just directing that such time be provided. This sense of phrasing appeared more unconscious than intentional; nonetheless, it was a regular and consistent pattern of behavior for these teams.

Building on the other's ideas often took the form of finishing one another's thoughts or sentences. At times, a teacher would take an idea to a certain degree, and his or her voice would trail off as he or she searched for the next piece of the puzzle. At this point, it was common for the partner to pick up where the other left off in mid-sentence and to extend that idea one step further.

As Erica and Shannon shared their vision of the children's book project with the special educator on their team, this building process became increasingly evident. As they related the steps of constructing the books, they traded off—Shannon explained the illustrations and Erica moved from that to discuss how the text might interact with the visuals on a page. As they spoke, the project gradually evolved into a whole.

Hope and Krista worked on their upcoming Explorers Unit in their Monday planning meeting and began to build a structure for the week. "First we could determine why they wanted to come to America..." Hope began. "And then we could actually dress up like a Spaniard or a French person...", Krista added. "And that could be the second day...", Hope built further. This layering of ideas served to enrich the final product as they planned.

These team members also tended to reinforce their partners, underscoring what each one said or did. Most often, this reinforcement took the form of echoing directions or expectations to the students on the team. Particularly in these wide, double classrooms where it was oftentimes difficult to project, repeating directions was a helpful habit.

As Erica and Shannon prepared to inform their eighth-grade class about the structure of the math test, Shannon announced, "We're going to do our math test today in family groups." A split second passed, and Erica echoed the information from the other side of the room. Later, as they instructed the students to spread out, they switched roles unconsciously, and Shannon played the role of the reinforcer.

At times, however, the reinforcing was more than merely reiterating to students; it sometimes included encouraging and praising a teammate for actions or words. After Krista voiced her concern to their administrator regarding a recent decision he had made, Hope praised her for doing so. In this manner, she let Krista know that she supported her point of view and the action she had taken.

During planning meetings, one of the partners would often serve informally as the summarizer, systematically repeating the delineation of responsibilities. This clarification of roles served to safeguard against the possibility of miscommunication. After the teachers had agreed upon tasks each would accomplish, Krista clarified, "So, I'll continue to research the French and Spanish explorers and let you know what I find. I'll take the lead on the magazine's mandatory assignments, and you'll do the electives." As Krista reviewed the responsibilities they had agreed to, she lessened the chance for misunderstanding between them.

Returning to the children's book project, Erica and Shannon also found that summarizing their roles was a natural and helpful component of their planning process. After explaining the process to the special educator, Erica offered, "I'm in charge of the story; Shannon is in charge of the construction and binding." Because of the strong foundation of trust and respect upon which these partnerships were built, the teachers felt accepted when voicing their concerns. Each knew he or she would be heard with an open mind.

After experiencing a miscommunication regarding the planning of an integrated unit, Hope returned to a potentially uncomfortable conversation, with the goal of "clearing the air." Sensing that her actions threw Krista off somewhat, Hope turned to Krista. "I feel like I threw you a monkey wrench," she said compassionately. "I don't want to put any undue stress on you." Hope's ability to be up front about her feelings enabled the partners to address the issue and move on. Often, being candid about emotions did not necessarily relate directly to the relationship between the two teachers.

Shannon introduced a topic at their morning planning meeting with the special educator on their team. "Should we talk about the picture issue or not?" Shannon asked, referring to a discipline issue that has recently arisen with a student on their team. "I'd rather not," Erica admitted honestly, "I don't want to throw out too many things today. I'm just not up for it."

Being honest about areas of concern allowed these teachers to be clear with each other about their own boundaries and when a boundary was crossed. As Krista and Hope continued to plan their unit, their responsibilities rose. At a certain point, Hope was clear with her limits, "I'd like to be able to take this over and say, 'Don't worry about it,' but I'm going to feel incredibly swamped if I assume more of this."

These boundaries applied to skills as well as time, and to guarding as well as extending boundaries. The teachers were clear about each other's skill levels and knew what they each needed to accomplish and learn. Alan spoke of needing to extend his own boundaries as he and Heather discussed preparing report cards. "Guess I'd better make up the rank card!" Alan stated. "No, I'll type it up for you," Heather was quick to offer; but Alan refused, assuring her that he needed to learn how to do it better himself.

These partner teachers worked so closely together that many of their resources were combined. From grading and record keeping, to individual student files, to teaching resources, these classrooms tended to have an abundance of three-ring binders or folders, which were jointly created and maintained by the teachers. In some cases, they served to keep communication ongoing, as in a job-share situation. In others, they provided a holding ground for ideas and materials they would eventually discuss in planning meetings. In still others, these materials served as the artifacts of teaching, to return to time and again.

For John and Ted, a joint three-ring binder held the team's files on students. In it, they placed individual education plans, minutes from instructional support team meetings, parent conference information, and other student-specific notes. They also kept a separate binder for each of the integrated, thematic units that they taught, clearly labeled with titles such as Solar System, Voyage of the Mimi II, and Ocean Rescue.

Heather and Alan used a common filing system as well. As they jotted down notes throughout the week to prepare for their weekly school planning meeting, they placed them in a mutual folder. They then referred to this folder to create an agenda each Friday based on both of their needs and observations.

Krista and Hope employed a similar method for filing their everyday concerns. In addition, they kept an ongoing folder in between their desks for ideas related to the upcoming unit. As the time draws closer to the unit, they pull out the folder to use in creating their next unit.

The final behavioral tendency noted was the common use by teachers in this study of the pronoun "we" in ways that were atypical of normal usage. When Alan and Heather met in their weekly meeting, Alan asked, "Do we know anything about the arts and crafts thing yet?" thereby suggesting that for her alone to know would be sufficient. In addition to this notion of collective team knowledge was the concept of collective team will. As Erica and Shannon worked together on assessing one student's project, Shannon inquired, "So, do we want to do the same percentage we did with the other project?" Later in the day, explaining a successful assignment to another teacher, Erica stated, "We knew we had succeeded when they did that." Both cases exemplify their use of the pronoun "we" to communicate a collective will or desire.

Overall, these patterns of relational behavior suggested that these effective partner teams have negotiated and established ways of relating among themselves and their students, enabling the teachers to function smoothly as a team.

Leadership responsibilities

While team members bear a responsibility for acting in ways that promote the health and longevity of the team, the administrator involved also plays a critical role in ensuring its success. The leadership role assumed by the principal substantially influences team functioning. Teachers on highly effective teams report that their ability to perform well as individuals and as team members is enhanced by a supportive and understanding principal (Maeroff, 1993).

Knowing the stages of team development is critical information for a principal. Arbuckle and Murray (1989) provide one of the most widely accepted stage theories of team development. They found that all teams go through a five stage process: 1. Orientation Stage —*Forming*; 2. Dissatisfaction Stage—*Storming*; 3. Resolution Stage —*Norming*; 4. Production Stage—*Performing*; 5. Termination. Understanding that team development is an evolving, changing process helps a principal guide and encourage a partner team through the more challenging stages of development.

> Groups of people working together do not become a team in a day. Teams evolve and become productive over time. During this process, some of the activities and feelings of the team members may not appear to be productive. This is particularly true during the dissatisfaction stage when a sense of frustration and incompetence frequently emerges. However, working

through each stage is a crucial part of the team's
evolution if the end result is to be a fully functional
team. (Arbuckle & Murray, pp. 6-59)

Yvonne's and Lori's initial fears about undertaking partner
teaming were allayed because their principal understood the stages
of team development and was able to provide support during crucial
periods. Lori recalls,

> Our principal really trusted and supported us when we
> started out. The first to do this at our school, we were
> more than frightened. There were times when we felt
> stuck and frustrated, but she was always there assuring
> us that what we were experiencing was just what
> should be happening. It gave us comfort to know we
> were normal.

The teachers were clear in advising principals to allow teams the
time and support needed while they evolved at their own pace.

It is also important that principals balance their support between
team identity and the efforts of individual teachers. The principal
needs to understand that individuals maintain a distinct sense of self
even while becoming a part of a team. While principals must support
the team as a whole, they must also recognize the individuality and
uniqueness of each teacher. Effective teams require both collective
and individual feedback if they are to be productive and successful.
Evaluations should be two-tiered to include individual as well as
team evaluations. Unfortunately, very few teams receive supervisory
or evaluative feedback in this manner.

Principals must also understand the demands and level of
commitment required of partner teams and stand ready to articulate,
defend, and advocate when necessary. Principals must provide
common meeting time, shared space, a flexible, blocked schedule,
and access to professional development. Administrators who
understand and advocate for these needs and build support among
their communities and boards move beyond the role of the manager
to offer true leadership.

Professional development

Most professional development opportunities for teachers occur off-site through workshops, professional conferences, and graduate level courses. While the teachers on partner teams take advantage of these opportunities, their professional development is ongoing as the two teachers interact with each other throughout the day, learning and growing through their continual exposure to the other's teaching. The teachers in our study regularly learned concepts about a subject area that had previously been weak or unclear for them. They saw new connections among areas of the curriculum and could develop units or activities to support these connections. One team, for example, developed a major unit on genetics that linked the science and math curriculum, evolving from conversations about two previously unconnected units. The result was a new genetics unit and increased content knowledge for both teachers.

Constant exposure to a partner's teaching expanded one's own repertoire of skills and approaches. These collaborative exchanges between the teachers took place in the daily activity of the classroom, allowing students to see their teachers as learners and mentors to one another.

The importance of providing teachers with opportunities to constantly deepen their understanding of the content they teach is widely accepted.

> There is a strong reliable relationship between teachers' content knowledge and the quality of their instruction. Teachers with a deep conceptual understanding of their subject ask a greater number of high-level questions, encourage students to apply and transfer knowledge, and make other choices in their instruction that engage students and challenge them to learn. (Rigden, 2000, p.1)

The complementary and diverse subject area strengths inherent in partner teams expand the opportunities for teachers to experience a broadening and deepening understanding of content area knowledge.

During their co-teaching, the teachers receive immediate and ongoing information from each other on the effectiveness of the lesson. This feedback often encompasses a whole range of teaching behaviors but frequently focuses on a specific area of concern, such as clarity of instruction. The teacher then could immediately adjust her or his approach. If the adjustments are successful, the teacher receives immediate reinforcement and can apply this new learning to subsequent lessons. The value of teachers who grow as they work together every day is strongly supported in current research.

While the improvement of instruction can occur through training, coaching, critical friends' groups, study groups, and other reflective processes, one of the most obvious and direct ways to improve teaching is to have teachers continuously work with others to improve the quality of their lessons and examine student work to determine whether those lessons are assisting all students to achieve at high levels (Sparks, 2002, p. 97).

Professional development on partner teams is not a monthly or quarterly event but rather a daily one. It occurs as part of the natural course of the everyday interactions within the classroom between the teachers as well as among the students. The partner team provides teachers with the ongoing support and opportunity for practice necessary for the daily improvement of instructional practices that will improve student achievement.

Time

Time, or the lack of it, is frequently cited as a barrier to the reflection and discussion necessary to determine the quality and effectiveness of teaching. Our research was no exception. Krista explains, "It's time. Time is the biggest thing. I think we could do magic if we have an hour a day set aside just for us to talk about what is happening."

The partner teachers are quick to point out that partner teaming is much more time-consuming than their previous teaming arrangements. Finding time to plan, creating time to share and nurture the personal side of the partner relationship, and balancing other commitments such as family are all challenges for these teachers, an essential requirement of their effectiveness. Krista spoke of how lack of time affected their program and all they would like to achieve.

> I think education is doing a huge disservice to kids in general by not giving us that time to work together. It's

been the thing that has caused us the most problems
in our relationship for seven years. It's not having the
time to spend working out a great curriculum for the
kids. It has prevented us from communicating more
with the public or with our parent community. It keeps
us from getting to know individuals better. It's time.

The time Shannon and Erica put into planning spoke to their
commitment to make their curriculum relevant to their students.
Although these two often planned together mornings, nights,
weekends, as well as commuting together, critical events often
stimulated them to be creative in making time where many might
not. Shannon recounted,

We have planned at 5:00 in the morning... we have
planned at night. The year the Gulf War broke out...
we were on the phone at 4:00 in the morning bagging
our curriculum and basically designing a new one to
fit the crisis. We had a child who had been in our core
group who had moved away a month earlier and was
now in the Gulf area.

In addition to the time spent together planning curriculum, these
teachers pointed to the practice of spending time personally sharing
with one another as an element contributing to their effectiveness.
Krista offered,

We need to help that personal part stay really strong
and grow. So, Hope supports me a lot in my marathon
run. She loves horses and gardening, and I am always
looking for way that I can bring in something for her
that will enhance these interests.

Krista also spoke of what occurs when time for nuturing personal
concerns was simply not available.

I think this year, in particular, with all the things that
have happened with the student teacher and some
other risks that we took, that we have had a lot more
instances where we have almost fought and gotten
angry with one another real quick. It has taken my
breath away and hers too, and we realized in order for
us to be all that we can be... we have to have some

time as persons. And when we don't get it, we are not as powerful.

The crucial role the principal plays in providing the time necessary to maintain a healthy vibrant team culture is clear. Teachers and administrators both have to be held accountable for a team's success. When both the teachers and principal assume joint responsibility for the health and welfare of the team, many positive outcomes result. ⊚

6

CONCLUSIONS AND CONSIDERATIONS: WHAT'S IMPORTANT?

The dogmas of the quiet past are inadequate to the stormy present…as our case is new, so we must think anew and act anew. — Abraham Lincoln

Listening to partner team teachers and students tell their stories is illuminating. The fine examples of collaborative work that filled our research made evident the extraordinary possibilities of teaming. Of all of the reform efforts employed in American schools over the past decade, teaming is surely one of the most powerful. It has the capacity to transform the way schools function for both teacher and student. Teaming enables a level of collaboration that simply cannot exist when teachers are isolated entities. Much more than an organizational arrangement or an instructional innovation, teaming can dramatically shift the culture of a school and what the humans therein experience.

It is tempting to try to construct a recipe for successful teams for others to replicate: one part humor, two parts common work ethic, five parts complementary strengths, and so forth. The reality, however, is that teams are highly dependent upon the players and the ways those players interact. A unique chemistry exists among them. As the vignettes and quotes in this book portray, the subtle differences between teams is an important reminder that there is no prescription or recipe for success. It is the individual nature of these teams that makes them work. For example, while most teamed actively over the course of the day, Erica and Shannon spent only the morning together. While most teams had a dividing wall open all day between two classroom spaces, Heather and Alan appeared to rely more heavily on their individual spaces. Each team made programmatic decisions based on student population and needs. This individuality contributed to a team's successes and its effectiveness.

At the same time, however, each team displayed similar attributes and used processes that were central to its effectiveness, thereby revealing much to those of us interested in creating and maintaining effective partner teams. The real recipe for success lies in the mix of these generally agreed upon common factors blended with customized approaches. From a solid foundation, teams built an individual and unique structure. Each of the partner teams represented here is synergistic; the whole is more than the sum of its parts. On these teams, one could say, 1+1=3—or more.

Learning from partner teams about effective collaborative work necessarily raises other questions about schooling for young adolescents and the professional lives of their teachers. Because the distinct aspects of middle level reform efforts are inherently intertwined, the practice of teaming cannot be artificially separated from other important change efforts in schools. In fact research revealing significant student outcomes in schools implementing the *Turning Points* recommendations (Felner et al.,1997) reminds us that such reforms must be implemented as a whole, rather than as a discrete set of parts, to be most effective. The position paper of National Middle School Association (2003) says specifically,

> Perhaps the most profound and enduring lesson learned in 30 years of active middle school advocacy is that the several distinct elements of successful middle level schools work best as parts of the larger whole.... Schools should not choose among characteristics, implementing only those that appear to be more achievable or seem more appropriate for a school or a particular situation. Rather, successful middle level schools recognize that the 14 characteristics described in *This We Believe: Successful Schools for Young Adolescents* are interdependent and must be implemented in concert. (p. 2)

Our research raises questions about the myriad other aspects of best middle level practice that exist in schools. For example, as discussed in Chapter 3, partner teams present important alternatives to how we meet the fundamental goals of teacher advisory. Our findings cause us to think differently not only about forming and strengthening effective teams, but about other matters, including advisory, relevant to middle schools. What are the implications of partner teaming for the whole system of middle level schooling? Here we consider such issues: How are the teams inclusive of all learners? How can the physical plant be conducive to collaborative work? How can policy play a role in supporting such collaborative frameworks? How might this inform teacher preparation in colleges and universities? How can relationships between teams be collaborative rather than competitive?

Reaching all learners

Without question, the national middle level education agenda is concerned with issues of equity. The vision statement of the National Forum to Accelerate Middle-Grades Reform is one of several position papers that call for schools with middle grades to offer equitable opportunity: "High-performing schools with middle grades are socially equitable. They seek to keep their students' future options open. They have high expectations for all their students and are committed to helping each child produce work of high quality..." (cited in Jackson & Davis, 2000, p.12). These words necessarily raise questions about how to serve all students well in the classroom, how to translate the rhetoric into reality. Certainly, at all levels of schooling there is currently great debate around how to effectively differentiate instruction to serve a diverse student body (Gregory & Chapman, 2001; Heacox, 2001; Tomlinson, 1999). Within the realm of special education, in particular, the movement from separate classrooms to a more inclusive approach for students with special needs represents a clear striving for equity and excellence in education for all students. With equity high on the national agenda, it is interesting to note the presence of a special educator working directly with some partner teams in our research. On several of the teams, the partner teachers worked with her (in these cases it was always a woman) very closely, and referred to her from time to time as a third member of their team. She was often involved as they divided the class into three groups, usually for math or spelling. In some cases, the special educator would take the highest groups, leaving the partners to work with those who needed more assistance. For the most part, she worked directly within the team, delivering services within the context of the regular class and not just to students identified as special education. These teams were rich models of incorporating a special educator as a team member in an inclusive, middle level classroom.

Physical space

"Geography matters." These wise words were spoken by one of the teachers on an effective partner team. He said them not in reference to his social studies curriculum, although he may have indeed believed it to be accurate for that as well. Rather, he was explaining the role that the physical plant played in facilitating effective teaming. Other partner teams identified physical space as a component of helping them do well what they do.

Unfortunately, very little research has explicitly examined the role of physical space in fostering collaborative work. These teams all had the benefit of an open, double classroom; and in the majority of them, this space could be separated by moveable dividers. The ability to have all of the team's students together in one space, as well as the potential to group them flexibly, was central to the teaching and learning that took place within the space. Since it was clear that ample and flexible space was a central component in partner teams, any middle level community considering partner teaming should examine the physical configurations available.

Policy

Middle level leaders play many roles, from possessing and articulating a developmentally responsive vision to organizing the educational community to carry out that vision. Those in positions of leadership are critical to the growth, health, and success of the middle school. With the partner teams in this study, it is particularly striking to note the "invisible leadership" perceived by many of these teams. When asked about the role that building level principals played in achieving their team goals, many teachers inferred that they were supported primarily by a lack of interference on the part of administration. They felt supported in their endeavors to attempt different curricular strategies or teaming approaches by being given permission to stretch themselves in new ways. Yet, often the role of leadership seemed to end at the permission-granting stage, leaving these partner teams primarily on their own to move further onto the middle level landscape.

These teachers did not voice this as a negative component of their teaming experience. As Heather noted, "Administration is supportive in that they don't say anything to us." This invisible leadership supported teams by not introducing conflict or barriers rather than by providing specific support or a vision that one would hope to receive from leadership. Sometimes, however, the non-interference moved into the realm of clashing with a team's philosophy, as when Krista challenged a principal's decision. In such cases, there is obvious tension that cuts into the energy and productivity of the team, as a lack of understanding or philosophical agreement thwarted a team's efforts.

This raises questions about the role of leadership in nurturing teams who are on the cutting edge of middle level education. The role of the administrator was examined in previous chapters as it pertains to forming and supporting teams. Yet, what happens for the teams who are at a high performing stage of development? As members of effective partner teams, these teachers are experimenting with new and innovative ways of providing developmentally responsive pedagogy to young adolescents. In many cases, their vision goes beyond that of their administrator's. What does this mean for the role of leadership? Research on effective middle schools asserts that a critical component is the leader's possession of a driving vision that helps lead others to manifest that vision. We suspect, therefore, that for a leader to support teams at all stages, he or she must fully understand the vision behind the tenets of *This We Believe: Successful Schools for Young Adolescents* (NMSA, 2003).

This focus on middle level philosophy that addresses the needs of young adolescents as unique and distinct is still relatively new. As an open attempt to move away from the junior version of high school, the middle level concept is a move toward developmentally responsive education. As with many restructuring efforts, middle level research and practices have progressed more quickly than the policies that surround them. In almost all states, for example, there is little incentive for administrators to become proficient in middle level philosophy, as administrators are primarily licensed K-12, with no course work or experience specific to the schooling of young adolescents required. There is a grave need for state departments of education to revamp the ways in which they license middle level administrators.

Teacher preparation

The partner team teachers in our study taught us important lessons about the preparation of future middle grades teachers. Those involved in pre-service teacher education play a special role in shaping the middle level classrooms of the future. Certainly, the core beliefs held by teacher educators translate into classroom practice, for better or worse. How do they, then, shape classroom experiences for future middle grades teachers? What attributes and dispositions will serve teachers best as they take on the responsibility of this highly collaborative work?

During the course of our project, a principal proudly announced to one of us that, "In our building, teaming is not an option. It is a job requirement." As one scans the national middle level landscape, it is clear that teaming is the preferred organizational arrangement. Most middle grades teachers work in collaborative environments. Modeling team planning and teaching within teacher preparation programs is an obvious way to prepare students for working together effectively. Further, it is not enough to merely offer students opportunities to work with one another; programs must be intentionally designed to help them learn the discrete skills of collaboration, interpersonal negotiation, and teamwork to set them up for success in that arena as the students complete complex and challenging tasks. Multiple field experiences that showcase effective teams also offer them opportunities to examine the practice in action and to learn from others' processes and modeling. In middle grades pre-service programs, it is no longer acceptable to use field placements that replicate the norm of teaching as an isolated act. Only situations that exemplify the complex, collaborative, high quality work of teachers in the middle grades are acceptable.

Excellence as attainable for all

An additional finding of our study was of some concern. As the effective teams spoke of their successes, they also told tales of dissonance in their building or district between teams, of inter-team isolation. Research on teaming suggests that personal isolation is greatly reduced within a team teaching situation, but it also recognizes that subject matter and inter-team isolation occur. On each of these teams, the partners experienced varying degrees of both content area and inter-team isolation.

Within their school, for example, Erica and Shannon spoke of a "war" with the departments within which they worked. In short, the subject departments to which they had long belonged were resistant to the establishment of the partner team. For this school, to be a part of a team was to not be part of a department. For Erica and Shannon, however, it was a clean break; although they still attended meetings, their first loyalties lay with the team. This break was not without personal and professional sacrifices in relationships, however.

While Erica and Shannon struggled with subject matter isolation as a part of a 7-12 system, partner team members in other school configurations described inter-team isolation at play. The relationships between teams were often strained, for a variety of reasons.

Several of the longest operating teams had received a level of notoriety for their practices in middle level teaming. One team, for example, had been the subject of a video, another the subject of a nationally published monograph. In each case, they experienced a fair amount of animosity within the school regarding their practices and the ways in which these practices strayed from the cultural norms of the school or district. This "super-team syndrome" caused a breakdown in relationships between teams and among colleagues. As Alan illustrates, "Once the monograph came out, and we started getting invited to national conferences to present, I sensed jealousy. They couldn't understand why we were getting recognition, and that caused a problem." The level of notoriety on the part of these effective teams often resulted in a chasm with other teams in their buildings, resulting in extreme inter-team isolation.

Bryk and Schneider (2002) wrote of the importance of "relational trust" in implementing school reform efforts that raise student achievement. Their research contended that schools with strong levels of trust at the outset of reforms had a one in two chance of making significant improvements in math and reading, while those with weak relationships stood a one in seven chance of making such progress (Gordon, 2002). Given that many schools are organized in ways that inhibit collaborative work, with little or no time provided for teachers to communicate and plan together, these are important findings indeed. While the partner team is fundamentally based on trust, an interesting and significant issue with regard to inter-team relationships emerges. How might we take what we learn from these powerful teams and spread the highly collaborative practices, without alienating other educators in the process? Beginning to define excellence as attainable for all, rather than viewing it as a limited commodity, is a critical step in creating effective teams. Designating one team as effective should not reduce the possibilities of others' efficacy, but inevitably it does.

One step toward excellence for all teams was the promotion of active reflection as a means of embedded professional development. The partner team is a prime example of ongoing, systemic learning for teachers as they question and reflect on their practices. These teachers recognized the professional growth that occurred. It is interesting to note this finding in light of the literature that describes the potentially dangerous effect of strong professional communities, where members tend to reinforce internal beliefs rather than question the practices of the group (Hargreaves, 1993). On the one hand, the partners were breaking away from strong departmental allegiances, while on the other hand, they entered into an even more intimate loyalty in the partner team. From Hargreaves' study, one might anticipate this loyalty to result in the reinforcement of existing internal beliefs, yet these teams describe the active role reflection plays in promoting critical questioning between the two partners and a readiness to try new things.

Teaching as sustaining work

Many of the teachers in our research were veterans in their field, with their years of teaching experience ranging from seven to 26. Although they were quick to point out that this type of teaming demanded more energy and time than their previous teaching arrangements, these partners highlighted the benefits that teaming afforded them and were uniform in their belief that they were both more satisfied and better teachers as a result. In a field where teachers most often leave the profession claiming to be "burned out" due to stress, depersonalization, and status dissatisfaction (Friesen, 1988), the exuberance and enthusiasm of these teachers were striking and encouraging. They attributed this attitude to their teaming experience, calling to the table a multitude of implications for the organization of teaming. The benefits they delineated were a product of a partnership that was sustaining and reinvigorating.

The teachers presented here pushed themselves to work above and beyond a typical workload, planning together before and after the school day, sometimes on weekends, and even during the summer. They worked hard to collaborate, often at the expense of personal and family time. What enabled them to work to this degree and still be refreshed? McLelland and Franz's study on caregiving as a "calling" (1993) suggested that those who reported being called by God into the profession of caregiving did not experience the high levels of burnout rate that "professional" caregivers did. Through their faith, these caregivers were dedicated and refreshed in their work. They found strength in their faith to continue work that required immense time, energy, and emotion. For the caregivers in McLelland and Franz's study, "...because the helping transaction in itself is joyous, they do not burn out" (p.283). Is the partner relationship the corollary to the caregiver's God, serving as that entity in which to place faith, to have hope, and to find support? Certainly, the teachers in our research reported tremendous support and joy as a result of their teaming. Krista offered, "The partner team has kept me just as excited about teaching after 23 years as I was after 10 years." Erica's words revealed a similar theme, "I go to conferences where most of the people are my age, and I hear them talk about looking forward to retirement because current conditions in education appear to lead to a dead end. For us, every day is a new day, a new opportunity."

The 16 teachers in this study presented a most positive perspective. Partner teaming can be both isolating and time-intensive work, and one is often bombarded with demands well beyond the everyday instructional aspects of educating students. While trying to be attentive to various needs around them, teachers can become overwhelmed by all they should be doing for students. Yet, the teachers in this study experienced a profound sense of efficacy and continued to be excited about teaching.

In her ethnographic study of youths who are doing work they love, Munoz (1995) discusses Luther's concept of *opera manum Dei* (the hands that do the work of God). This construct of love and work as a combination in life, she puts forth, is life sustaining; it confirms the very identity of these youths. In this era where education is often held up as failing, many teachers leave teaching to seek other employment. National concern about the teacher shortage has more recently been redefined as one of teacher retention not just recruitment. "The fact is, an alarming and unsustainable number of teachers are leaving teaching during their first few years of teaching." (National Commission on Teaching and America's Future, 2002, p. 3) Yet, for the partner teams in this study, teaching holds rewards far beyond what most enjoy. How is it that they live so fully through their professions? This group of teachers speaks to the world of possibilities they have found; it is a world of support and professional growth, of flexibility and risk taking. Perhaps most importantly, it is a world of true enjoyment in their profession. It is a love of work; it is work of love. ©

AFTERWORD—ADVICE FROM THE AUTHORS

A letter to teachers

Teaming is hard work. Understanding the personality and philosophy of a teammate, planning collaboratively and well, and accommodating another's needs take time and energy. All of these things require more work than does teaching solo. Yet, for all of this hard work, in partner teams teachers reap untold benefits of personal and professional support and reinvigoration. And, most importantly, students gain too. So, if you're a teacher considering partner teaming, how can you help to ensure success?

First, consider anew what you believe about teaching middle level learners. Reflect on the tremendous potential of teaming in general and partner teaming in particular. If you are convinced that making connections between and among disciplines is important to teaching this age group, if you enjoy collaborative endeavors, if you approach your work with this age group with passion and deep commitment, if you have been frustrated by the isolation of your classroom and the continuing struggle for consensus among four or five teammates, then you may be a good prospect for a partner team.

Next, look around, look for a partner with whom you would really like to work. Having a voice in who your teammate will be is the key to your team's success. Talk with other teachers about their perspectives on teaching and learning. Invite them to share their hopes for middle level learners and for what goes on in their classrooms. Observe their styles of teaching and relating to colleagues. Are they complementary to yours? Do they have a common commitment to this work, and do they have a similar amount of time and energy to dedicate? Together, if possible, visit a school to see a partnership in action.

Concurrently, build a core of support for this practice. Discuss the possibility with the school's administration to ascertain what support you would have from leadership. Anticipate the arguments against such an initiative, and be ready to have solid, well-conceived responses. Knowing fewer students well and working with a compatible colleague really can translate into powerful practices that can be described. Talk with parents and families who might like to have a smaller community of learning for their children, and advocate for the smaller team in appropriate settings.

In advocating for the partner team, be mindful that long-term relationships are the backbone of the team. Students on the team are best served by the opportunity to build real, meaningful relationships with their teachers and peers over multiple years. This can be achieved through a multiage environment in which young adolescents of different ages and grades are intentionally placed together, where teachers and learners capitalize on the range of knowledge and skills in the group, and where graded distinctions are reduced. Long-term relationships are also built by looping, the process of teachers moving with students from one grade to the next. In both cases, teachers come to know students deeply, as learners and as people, in ways that one academic year simply does not allow.

Often, such teams may become possible when new hirings occur. If this is the case, advocate for your presence on the search committee, and be upfront with all members about your own styles and needs, clarifying which attributes, strengths, and content area expertise you would bring to a partnership.

Although it is sometimes impractical, spend as much time together as possible before launching a team with students. Take the time to develop a shared belief statement, and consider your team norms. One team we know that was going to be formed by splitting off from two interdisciplinary teams, spent a full year planning prior to their formation, working with the principal and colleagues to minimize the impact on current teams. Another team we know spends two or three days each summer in something of a retreat at a teammate's summer cottage. Good partner teams don't happen by accident. They require a lot of long-term planning and, then, ongoing attention.

Once the team is underway, communicate, communicate, communicate. It's tempting to think your teammate can read your mind; and over time, he or she may do that; but don't assume it. Take the time to ensure you have been heard, and, conversely, that you elicit your teammate's perspective continually. Recognize what he or she offers that is unique and honor that. Seek it out, and value it. Similarly, offer enough of yourself to be known as both a person and a professional.

Value your time together as well. It's tempting, in the ongoing craziness of the school day, to sacrifice common planning time to assess student work or make those phone calls, but thoughtful and reflective time devoted to connecting and mutual planning is essential. Take the initiative to ensure that your partner team sits down together regularly, moves forward on the mutual agenda, summarizing roles and responsibilities along the way. At the same time, remember to share the small and large victories together, and to laugh together. The teams we studied convinced us that humor is critical to effective collaborative work.

Partner teams are one of the most exciting proposals in the current middle level reform effort. They have such obvious benefits, and in the hands of two philosophically compatible professionals, educational magic occurs.

A letter to administrators

While our study identified one form of administrative support simply as non-interference, we strongly believe that taking a proactive approach will best serve the teachers as well as the students on a school's partner team. As you contemplate developing partner teams in your middle school or supporting one that already exists, there are a number of factors to consider that will help a partner team grow and thrive.

First, allow for team self-selection. These two individuals will spend the majority of their working day, and often some time outside of school together. They must feel as confident as possible that the arrangement will be professionally and personally fulfilling. Teams, whether in education, business, or industry, who self-select, have a greater commitment to the team and spend significant time engaged in team planning and coordination—actions necessary for an ongoing successful teaming situation. Due to state licensing requirements, you may have to seek a waiver to allow a team to be formed that doesn't match normal certification requirements.

Adhering to several criteria that we have found to be critical when forming a partner team will help ensure success. Every one of the 16 teachers in our study identified a common belief system about teaching and learning as the single most important criterion for selecting a partner. Their philosophy formed the bedrock of all their actions with each other, with students, parents, colleagues, and with the larger school community. Their advice was clear: "Don't even think about a partnership unless the philosophy is aligned."

Compatible personalities and complementary teaching styles were also critical in team selection, for obvious reasons. Teachers inevitably participate in ongoing professional development as they observe one another and discuss the success of their plans. Though partner teams deal with only 40 to 50 students, the teachers are nonetheless responsible for all of the core subjects as well as the same administrative responsibilities found on larger teams. This translates into time both before and after school. Ensuring that both team members have a common work ethic is crucial if the team is to stay on an even keel and meet all of its obligations.

Once the team is formed and functioning, don't assume that your work is over; it has just begun. If the partner team is a new teaming configuration in your school, communicating the similarities and differences in relation to your larger teams to other teams, parents, other administrators, and board members is an important responsibility. There is a high level of commitment required on a partner team that can differ significantly from larger teams and as the principal you must be willing and able to articulate, defend, and advocate for the resulting needs of this relationship to the whole school community. Your strong understanding of the partner team's philosophy and desired outcomes for its students, along with how this approach reflects best middle school practice, will enhance the effectiveness of your communication. If you can portray the partner team as a choice on a continuum of teaming possibilities, necessary to meet the varied needs of all learners, you will go a long way toward preventing inter-team rivalries and promoting healthy, functional cross-team relationships.

As with all of the teams in your building, ongoing, regular communication with a partner team is essential to ensure that you're aware of both its successes and challenges. Don't make the mistake of assuming that somehow since there are only two teachers they require less of your time and attention than your larger teams. The fact that two teachers must meet the same administrative and teaching obligations, albeit with fewer students, is a strong reason for you to monitor them at least as closely as other teams. Because there are only two teachers, your actual contact time may be less, but the number of times you meet with them should be comparable to your larger teams.

There are additional factors that, while not essential, will greatly enhance and support the collaborative nature of a partner team. The first is the general proximity of the two teachers. This was achieved by the teams in our study in a variety of ways: 1. a completely open space large enough to house two class groups; 2. two classrooms separated by a folding wall; 3. two classrooms adjacent to one another connected by a single door; 4. classrooms directly across the hall from one another. Proximity allows for quick communications about changes in schedule, facilitates whole group activities, and enables easy divisions into smaller groups with a minimal amount of transition time.

Another factor is the schedule. Providing the partner team with a large academic block promotes the type of curriculum integration so important to the team. This extended period of time, coupled with the fact that the two teachers are responsible for all four subjects, allows for in-depth exploration and integration of the curriculum. The schedules, of course, must also provide teachers with a block of planning time that is so essential for realizing the possibilities of a partner team.

While the quality of students' experience on a partner team is largely dependent upon the talent, dedication, and energy of the two teachers, the teachers' ability to deliver a high quality program day after day depends on your support, understanding, and advocacy of the challenge they have assumed. They cannot do it alone. Your role in their work is essential for the long-term life of the partner team. ©

REFERENCES

Adams, L., & Cessna, K. (1993). Metaphors of the co-taught classroom. *Preventing School Failure, 37*(4), 28-31.

Aikin, W.M. (1942). *The story of the Eight-Year Study.* New York: Harper.

Alexander, W.M. (1995). 2-teacher teams promote integrative curriculum. *Middle Ground,* 4-6.

Allen-Malley, M., and Bishop, P. (2000, April). The power of partners: Two teacher teams. *Schools in the Middle.*

Arbuckle, M.A., & Murray, L.B. (1989). *Building systems for professional growth: An action guide.* Regional Laboratory for Educational Improvement of the Northeast and Islands. Augusta, ME: Maine Department of Educational and Cultural Services.

Arhar, J.M. (1994). Personalizing the social organization of middle-level school: Does interdisciplinary teaming make a difference? In K.B. Borman & N.P. Greenman (Eds.), *Changing American education: Recapturing the past or inventing the future?* (pp. 325-350). Albany, NY: SUNY.

Arnold, J., & Stevenson, C. (1998). *Teacher's teaming handbook: A middle level planning guide.* New York: Harcourt Brace.

Ashton, P.T., & Webb, R.B. (1986). *Making a difference: Teachers' sense of efficacy and student achievement.* New York: Longman.

Baltzer, R. (1995). Two-teacher teaming: Relationships and ownership. *The Journal of the New England Middle Schools, 8*(2), 16-18.

Baumrind, D. (1991). Parenting styles and adolescent development. In A.C. Petersen & J. Brooks-Gunn (Eds.), *The Encyclopedia on Adolescence* (pp. 758-772). New York: Garland.

Beane, J. (1997). *Curriculum integration: Designing the core of democratic education.* New York: Teachers College Press.

Bishop, P., & Stevenson, C. (2000). When smaller is greater: Two or three person partner teams. *Middle School Journal, 31*(3) 12-17.

Britton, T. (2002). *Comprehensive teacher induction: Systems for early career learning*. San Francisco, CA: WestEd.

Bryk, A.S., & Schneider, B. (2002*). Trust in schools: A core resource for improvement*. New York: Russell Sage.

Bunte, A.A. (1995). *Success factors in the implementation of advisory programs in selected Illlinois middle schools*. Unpublished doctoral dissertation, Southern Illinois University, Carbondale.

Butler, K. (1986). *Learning and teaching style: In theory and practice*. Columbia, CT: The Learner's Dimension.

Carnegie Council on Adolescent Development. (1989). *Turning points: Preparing American youth for the 21st century*. New York: The Carnegie Corporation.

Carnegie Council on Adolescent Development. (1995). *Great transitions: Preparing adolescents for a new century*. New York: Carnegie Corporation.

Connors, N.A. (1986). *A case study to determine the essential components and effects of an advisor/advisee program in an exemplary middle level school*. Unpublished doctoral dissertation, Florida State University, Tallahassee.

Council for Exceptional Children. (1993). *Including students with disabilities in general education classrooms*. Reston, VA: Author. (ERIC Document Reproduction Service No. ED 385 677).

Darrel, R., & Bronstein, H. (1995). *Teaming up: Making the transition to a self-directed team based organization*. New York: R.R. Donelly & Sons.

Dewey, J., & Dewey, E. (1962). *Schools of tomorrow*. New York: E.P. Dutton.

Dickinson, T., & Erb, T. (Eds.) (1997). *We gain more than we give: Teaming in middle schools*. Columbus, OH: National Middle School Association.

Dryfoos, J. (1998). *Safe passage: Making it through adolescence in a risky society*. New York: Oxford University Press.

Epstein, J.L., & Mac Iver, D.J. (1990). *Education in the middle grades: National practices and trends*. Columbus, OH: National Middle School Association.

Felner, R.D., Jackson, A.W., Kasak, D., Mulhall, P., Brand, S., & Flowers, N. (1997). The impact of school reform for the middle years: Longitudinal study of a network engaged in *Turning Points*-based comprehensive school transformation. *Phi Delta Kappan, 78*, 528-532, 541- 550.

Flowers, N., Mertens, S., & Mulhall, P. (2000). What makes interdisciplinary teams effective? *Middle School Journal, 31*(6), 53-56.

Friend, M., & Cook, L. (1992). *Collaboration skills for school professionals*. White Plains, NY: Longman.

Friesen, D. (1988). Why teachers burn out. *Educational Research Quarterly, 12*(3) 9-19.

Garbarino, J. (1997). Educating children in a socially toxic environment. *Educational Leadership, 54(7)*, 12-16.

Georgia Alliance for Middle Level Excellence. (n.d.). *Reforming Georgia's middle schools*. Milledgeville, GA: Author.

Gordon, D.T. (2002). Fuel for reform: The importance of trust in changing schools. *Harvard Education Letter, 18*(4). Cambridge, MA: Harvard Graduate School of Education.

Gregoric, A.F. (1982). *An adult's guide to style*. Maynard, MA: Gabriel Systems.

Gregory, G., & Chapman, C. (2001). *Differentiated instructional strategies: One size doesn't fit all*. Thousand Oaks, CA: Corwin Press.

Hargreaves, A. (1993). Individualism and individuality: Reinterpreting the teacher culture. In J.W. Little & M. McLaughlin, M. (Eds.), *Teachers' work*. New York: Teachers College Press.

Harris, K. (1990). *Collaborative instruction in schools: Key principles*. Paper presented at the Conference of the Learning Disabilities Association of America. Anaheim, CA. (ERIC Document Reproduction Service No. ED 326 001).

Heacox, D. (2001). *Differentiating instruction in the regular classroom: How to reach and teach all learners, grades 3-12*. New York: Free Spirit Publishing.

Jackson, R., & Davis, G. (2000). *Turning points 2000. Educating adolescents in the 21st century.* New York: Teachers College Press.

Johnson, S.M. (1990). *Teachers at work: Achieving success on our schools.* New York: BasicBooks.

Kirby L., & Myers, K, (2000). *Introduction to type: A Guide to understanding.* Palo Alto, CA: Consulting Psychologist Press.

Kleinsmith, S., & Everts-Rogers, S. (2000). The art of followership. *School Administrators, 57,*(8), 35-38.

Klonskey, M. (2002). How smaller schools prevent school violence. *Educational Leadership, 59* (5), 65-69.

Lee, V.E., Dedrick, R.F., & Smith, J.B. (1991). The effects of the social organization of schools on teachers' efficacy and satisfaction. *Sociology of Education, 64,* 190-208.

Lee, V.E., & Smith, J.B. (1993). Effects of school restructuring on the achievement and engagement of middle-grades students. *Sociology of Education, 66*(3), 164-187.

Little, J.W. (1990). The persistence of privacy: Autonomy and initiative in teachers' professional relations. *Teachers College Record, 91*(4), 509-536.

Lounsbury, J.H., & Vars, G.F. (1978). A curriculum for the middle school years. New York: Harper and Row.

Mac Iver, D.J. (1990). Meeting the needs of young adolescents: Advisory groups, interdisciplinary teaching teams and school transition programs. *Phi Delta Kappan, 71,* 504-511.

Maeroff, G. (1993*). Team building for school change: Equipping teachers for new roles.* New York: Teachers College Press.

Maine Commission on Middle Level Education. (in press). *Report of the Maine Commission on Middle Level Education.* Augusta, ME: Author.

McLelland, D., & Franz, C. (1993). In D.J. Nygren & M.D. Ukeritis (Eds.), *Transformation and commitment: Dynamics of organizational and individual change.* New York: Praeger.

McPartland, J.M. (1987*). Balancing high quality subject matter instruction with positive teacher-student relations in the middle grades: Effects of departmentalization, tracking and block scheduling on learning environments.* Report #15, Baltimore, MD: The Johns Hopkins University.

Mills, R.A., Powell, R.R., & Pollack, J.P. (1992). The influence of interdisciplinary teaming on teacher isolation: A case study. *Research in Middle Level Education, 12*(2), 9-26.

Munoz, V. (1995).*Where something catches: Work, love, and identity in youth.* Albany, NY: State University of New York Press.

National Commission on Teaching and America's Future. (2002, August). *Unraveling the "teacher shortage" problem: Teacher retention is the key.* A Symposium of NCTAF and NCTAF State Partners, Washington D.C.

National Middle School Association. (1995*). This we believe: Developmentally responsive middle level schools.* Columbus, OH: Author.

National Middle School Association. (2003). *This we believe: Successful schools for young adolescents.* Westerville, OH: Author.

Noddings, N. (1992). *The challenge to care in schools: An alternative approach to education.* New York: Teachers College Press.

Office of Juvenile Justice and Deliquency Prevention. (1999). *National youth gang survey, 1996. OJJDP Summary.* Washington, DC: Department of Justice.

Olson, D. (1993). Circumplex model of marital and family systems. In F. Walsh (Ed.), *Normal family processes* (pp. 104-137). New York: The Guilford Press.

Rigden, D. (2000). Implications of standards for teacher preparation. *Basic education, 45*(3), 1-6.

Rosenholtz, S. J. (1985). Effective schools: Interpreting the evidence. *American Journal of Education.*

Sage, S. (1995). *The nature of the collaborative relationship of regular and special educators: A qualitative case study.* Unpublished doctoral dissertation, Ohio State University, Columbus.

Sillars, A.L. (1995). Communication and family culture. In M.A. Fitzpatrick & A.I. Vangelisti (Eds.), *Explaining family interactions* (pp. 375-395). Thousand Oaks, CA: Sage Publications.

Sparks, D. (2002). *Designing powerful professional development for teachers and principals.* Oxford, OH: National Staff Development Council.

Springer, M. (1994) *Watershed: A successful voyage into integrative learning.* Columbus, OH: National Middle School Association.

Stanberry, A.M. (1994). *Communication: Helping families adapt to developmental challenges.* Presentation at SECA Annual Meeting: New Orleans, LA.

Stevenson, C. (2002*) Teaching ten to fourteen-year-olds.* White Plains, New York: Longman.

Tomlinson, C.A. (1999). *Differentiated classroom: Responding to the needs of all learners.* Alexandria, VA: Association for Supervision and Curriculum Development.

Vander Ark, T. (2002). The case for small high schools. *Educational Leadership 59*(5), 55-60.

Van Hoose, J. (1991). The ultimate goal: AA across the day. *Midpoints, 2*(1), 1-7.

Vermont Middle Grades Task Force. (2001). *The middle still matters: A vision of education for Vermont's young adolescents.* Montpelier, VT: Vermont Department of Education.

Wolcott, H. (1994). *Transforming qualitative data: Description, analysis, and interpretation.* Thousand Oaks, CA: Sage Publications.

National Middle School Association

National Middle School Association, established in 1973, is the voice for professionals and others interested in the education and well-being of young adolescents. The association has grown rapidly and enrolls members in all 50 states, the Canadian provinces, and 42 other nations. In addition, 57 state, regional, and provincial middle school associations are official affiliates of NMSA.

NMSA is the only national association dedicated exclusively to the education, development, and growth of young adolescents. Membership is open to all. While middle level teachers and administrators make up the bulk of the membership, central office personnel, college and university faculty, state department officials, other professionals, parents, and lay citizens are members and active in supporting our single mission— improving the educational experiences of 10-15 year olds.

This open and diverse membership is a particular strength of NMSA's. The association publishes *Middle School Journal*, the movement's premier professional journal; *Research in Middle Level Education Online; Middle Ground, the Magazine of Middle Level Education; The Family Connection,* an online newsletter for families; *Classroom Connections,* a practical quarterly resource; and a series of research summaries.

A leading publisher of professional books and monographs in the field of middle level education, NMSA provides resources both for understanding and advancing various aspects of the middle school concept and for assisting classroom teachers in planning for instruction. More than 70 NMSA publications are available through the resource catalog as well as selected titles published by other organizations.

The association's highly acclaimed annual conference has drawn many thousands of registrants every fall. NMSA also sponsors many other professional development opportunities.

For information about NMSA and its many services, contact the association's headquarters office at 4151 Executive Parkway, Suite 300, Westerville, Ohio, 43081. TELEPHONE: 800-528-NMSA; FAX: 614-895-4750; INTERNET: www. nmsa.org.

The Power of Two:
Partner Teams in Action